CONTENTS

Sections on "How Not to Lose a Pet Budgie" and "Common Budgie Diseases" by Leon F. Whitney, DVM.

Photo Credits:
Dr. Herbert R. Axelrod; p. 123. Horst Bielfeld; p. 122. Harry V. Lacey; p. 2, 3, 5, 11, 14, 15, 18, 19, 22, 23, 26-31, 36, 37, 46, 52, 55, 59, 62, 63, 65, 73, 75, 81-83, 85, 88, 89, 94, 96-100, 102, 103, 105-107, 110, 111, 114, 118, 119. W. L. Miller; p. 56. Horst Mueller; p. 14, 15, 18, 19, 22, 23, 26, 27, 30, 31, 64, 98, 102-104, 106, 107, 110, 111, 114, 115, 118, 119, 127. J. E. Townsend; p. 58. Walter D. Verizzo; p. 49. R. A. Vowles; p. 6, 10. Wohlin; p. 84. Worldwide Photos; p. 34, 40.

Front Endpapers:
These commercial budgies are very colorful and provide a lot of enjoyment and satisfaction for the beginning fancier.

Back endpapers:
In addition to the proper feeding of the budgie, these birds should also have plenty of opportunity to exercise in order to prevent unhealthy weight gain. Toys that serve well as exercise stations are available at pet shops.

ISBN 0-87666-998-4

Distributed in the U.S. by T.F.H. Publications, Inc., 211 West Sylvania Avenue, P.O. Box 427, Neptune, N.J. 07753; in England by T.F.H. (Gt. Britain) Ltd., 13 Nutley Lane, Reigate, Surrey; in Canada to the book store and library trade by Beaverbooks, 953 Dillingham Road, Pickering, Ontario L1W 1Z7; in Canada to the pet trade by Rolf C. Hagen Ltd., 3225 Sartelon Street, Montreal 382, Quebec; in Southeast Asia by Y.W. Ong, 9 Lorong 36 Geylang, Singapore 14; in Australia and the South Pacific by Pet Imports Pty. Ltd., P.O. Box 149, Brookvale 2100, N.S.W., Australia; in South Africa by Valiant Publishers (Pty.) Ltd., P.O. Box 78236, Sandton City, 2146, South Africa; Published by T.F.H. Publications, Inc., Ltd., The British Crown Colony of Hong Kong.

Australian
Shell Parrakeets

By Earl Schneider & Dr. Matthew M. Vriends

The ideal normal green budgerigar. On the continent of Europe budgerigars are judged on the point system, while in British Isles and in America judging is done by comparison only.

These budgies are shown in the act of feeding each other, which they often do prior to mating; they are exhibiting the normal behavior of well cared-for birds.

At left is one of a series of plates, published in 1837-38, which John Gould, author of *Birds of Australia and the Adjacent Islands,* used to illustrate the type of work which would go into the folio he planned. The plate presents two males and a female, identified as *Nanodes undulatus* (Vigors and Horsefeld). Below: The budgerigar is the most popular bird in aviaries and is commercially bred in great quantities.

History of the Budgie

In 1840 a little hitchhiker from the "down under" country started on its travels around the world. The name "budgerigar," a corruption of a native word meaning good bird or good food, indicates that it was a tasty morsel in the diet of the Australian aborigines. Gould, the naturalist, introduced the bird into England and was also responsible for reclassifying the budgerigar as *Melopsittacus undulatus*. Previously it had been known scientifically as *Psittacus undulatus*.

Gould's brother-in-law, Charles Coxen, hand-reared the birds and in a few years they were bred in captivity. The keeping of Australian or "shell" parrakeets (budgies) as pets spread rapidly throughout Europe, particularly Belgium and Holland.

The ideal hen budgerigar. Note specifically the shape of the skull and the cere.

A well-developed opaline cobalt.

In Japan the little fellow became all the rage. It is said that the first blue keets were brought into Japan from England, that they were purchased by a nobleman as a gift for his sweetheart. The giving of these little birds as love tokens rapidly became popular, and very high prices were paid for them by the Japanese. The boom lasted from 1925 to 1928, then almost as suddenly, due to the Japanese government banning their importation, the high prices tumbled. Budgerigars, or "love birds" as they were commonly called, were still popular but at prices almost everyone could afford.

At one time it was believed that parrakeets had to be kept in pairs, that one left alone would pine away and die. This may be true in the case of an old bird which has mated and bred. A young bird, hand-tamed, and treated kindly, is happy with its human companions. Its sprightly manners and amusing antics are most endearing, its plumage is bright, its voice is pleasant, its disposition is good. The bird is hardy by nature, its manners are clean, its care is simple, and, in addition to all this, it can be taught to talk. Is it any wonder that America, too, has taken the little immigrant to its heart?

The budgerigar is still frequently called "love bird," but this name is incorrect. The true "love bird" is African in origin and is heavier than the keet, with a short, stubby tail.

The budgie has also been confused with the Java rice bird, often sold under the name of "Java love bird." This pretty little bird has much to recommend it, but the fact that it does not have a hooked parrot-type bill is evidence that it is not a member of the parrot family. Hawks, eagles and owls, to name a few, all have hooked bills but this does not make them parrots. An easy way to differentiate is by inspecting the upper mandible (upper part of the bill). In parrot family birds this is not fixed rigidly to the forehead, but is hinged and can be moved readily by the bird.

In Australia, parrakeets travel and nest in great flocks. Travellers tell of seeing them in such great numbers that the branches of the trees were literally covered with chattering birds. They nest in every available hollow in the trunks of trees. When the cavity is not large enough, the parent bird uses its powerful beak to scoop out the soft and rotting wood. The eggs, five to eight in number, are laid on the bare wood, no nesting material whatever being used.

In the evening the birds gather in tremendous flocks and travel to the nearby water courses to drink. There they may be seen by the thousands in the trees lining the bank, all patiently waiting their turn to drink.

Budgerigars may be found throughout Australia at different times of the year, although they avoid the coastal area except in periods of extreme drought. They are migratory birds so their movements are regulated by the seasons. From written accounts, they appear to breed twice a year. In June. they nest in northern Queensland. In September they appear in western New South Wales, where they start their second nest. Nomadic by nature, the flocks return to the same district for a number of years and then suddenly fail to return for some time. In their natural habitat, the green phase of the parrakeet prevails, although occasionally a yellow makes its appearance.

When the bird became so popular as a cage bird, many thousands were trapped each year. This took so great a toll that Australia placed a ban on further exports. Fortunately the birds breed so readily in captivity that there is no real need of depending on wild stock for pets. Contrary to popular belief, birds bred under controlled conditions are far superior in size and color and are healthier than wild birds.

Early descriptions of the birds by naturalists are colorful and informative. Take, for example, the following, published in New South Wales by Shaw in the year 1805.

THE UNDULATED PARRAKEET

Bill, hooked; upper mandible movable.

Nostrils, round, placed in the base of the bill.

Tongue, fleshy, broad, blunt at the end.

Legs, short, feet scansorial.

Specific character, etc.

"Long-tailed green parrakeet, undulated above with brown; the throat yellowish; with blue spots, and the tail feathers yellow on the base.

"The highly elegant species of parrakeet represented on the present plate in its natural size is an inhabitant of New Holland (Australia), and seems to have been hitherto undescribed.

"The upper parts of the bird, from the bill to the rump, are of a pale yellowish-green, beautifully crossed by numerous linear brown undulations which become gradually larger as they approach the back and shoulders. The wing feathers are brown, with pale olive-yellow edges; the underparts of the bird together with the rump are of an elegant pale green; the throat pale yellow, mottled on each side with a few small, deep blue scattered spots, accompanied by small black crescents; the tail is of a cuneated form and of a deep blue color, with a bright yellow bar running obliquely across all feathers except the two middle ones, which consistently exceed the rest in length; the bill and legs are brown."

Later, Gould, in his *Birds of Australia and Adjacent Islands* (Pt. 1, plate 5, August, 1837), wrote:

"A single example of the female of this elegant little Parrot has been for

Opaline violet. The most difficult achievement in opaline breeding is to produce birds with as clear a mantle as possible and a clear "V" (the area on the back between the wings) and, at the same time, to hold the full markings on the wings.

Cinnamon light blue budgerigar. In the nest, cinnamon chicks display a reddish cinnamon through the closed eyelid before the eyes have opened. The feet are quite pink, and the down of the youngsters is either white or yellow.

many years in the collection of the Linnean Society; two other collections are referred to by Dr. Latham as containing specimens. It is only within the last few years that the male has become known. It was discovered in the greatest abundance by Captain Stuart during his journey into the interior of New South Wales; and specimens were transmitted by him to the Zoological Society, together with many other interesting birds. This gentleman informed me that on the extensive plains bordering the Murrumbridgu, he met with this lovely species in immense flocks, feeding on the seeds and berries of the low stunted bushes called scrubs, so abundant in those countries.

"I have also received several individuals in a collection sent to me by Mr. C. Coxen, which he had procured to the north of the Hunter's River.

"In their habits all the members of this group are extremely quick and active, running on the ground with great facility much after the manner of the true *Platy cerci* or Ground Parrakeets, to which they are closely allied in affinity. The present species differs from all other members of the group in the round, drop-like markings of the cheeks and throat, in its rich green coloring and in the prolonged centre tail feathers. Of its nest, eggs, etc., nothing is known."

CHRONOLOGY

1794.   In *Zoology of New Zealand*, the naturalist Shaw gave the first written description of the bird he named *Psittacus undulatus.*

1831.   A single specimen of a budgerigar was exhibited in the Linnaean Society Museum in London.

1840.   John Gould, the naturalist, introduced the first living specimens into England. These were raised by his brother-in-law, Charles Coxen. Gould also published a description of their habits (*The Birds of Australia,* 1840) and reclassified them as *Melopsittacus undulatus,* the scientific name they bear today.

1855.   In Berlin, budgerigars were bred for the first time by Grafin von Schwerin.

1870-75. A light yellow mutation appears from the mating of a pair of green budgerigars. The first yellow-colored birds are recorded as having appeared in Europe. There appeared to have been two types, both a dark or normal eye and a red-eyed type occurring at the same time. Although the black-eyed type was fixed and is being bred to this time, the red-eyed disappeared.

1880-85. The first sky-blues were noticed on the continent. These birds were carefully bred. Today the blue is the most popular pet color in America.

1910.   Sky-blue budgerigars were exhibited in England.

1915.   The first dark-green birds appeared in France.

1916.   Olive-green birds were developed from the dark-green.

1920.   The first cobalt-colored birds were bred by crossing sky-blue with olive-green.

1918-25.   Gray-winged greens, originally called "Jades," were reported as mutations several times. By crossing these with the ordinary blue and white, the blue form of the gray-wing was established.

1931.   Cinnamons were produced in England, Austria, and Germany. Red-eyed fallows were reported in California in this year but died out.

1932.   Fallow mutations appeared in Germany and, a little later, in Australia and South Africa. Albino mutations appeared and were fixed in several countries.

1933.   The clear-wing appeared in Australia and a dominant form of gray. Opalines were bred in England and Australia, the latter from a green opaline hen which was caught in a wild state.

1935.   Yellow-faced blues appeared and a Danish fancier fixed a true breeding strain of pied budgerigars.

The Second World War interrupted to a great extent the normal development of the budgerigar. In England and Europe particularly, bird fanciers had neither time nor food to spare. Undoubtedly many new colors were lost through the inability of bird owners to care for their budgerigars.

The keeping of parrakeets in America was dealt a severe blow when a discriminatory federal regulation was passed, prohibiting the interstate shipment of psittacine birds of all types, as well as their importation. Fortunately for the hobby, the many friends of the budgerigar rallied to its defense, and the law has been modified.

Now the future looks bright indeed. Budgerigar societies are springing up all over the country. There are several fine national organizations. The little bird has been widely accepted throughout the nation as a pet. In numbers it rivals the dog and is increasing in popularity so rapidly that it may even surpass the canines by the time this book is in print.

Dominant pied gray budgerigar. Dominant pieds of obvious heredity can be recognized in the nest before the baby down covers the skull by the small pink island of skin on the back of the skull, surrounded by normal black-pigmented skin. When the down grows in, the pink area produces light feathering that forms the pied nape spot. Light flight feathers can be predicted by the presence of similar pinkness on the wings.

Light blue graywing budgerigar. The recessive factor which produces the greywing cuts down the dark pigmentation in the wings and striations, resulting in about half of the normal intensity. This factor dilutes the body color in equal proportion. Greywings can be bred in all colors and varieties except the pastels, which are recessive to greywing.

Careful selection is the key to success in breeding your budgies. Enthusiastic as you may be in establishing your new hobby, though, don't overdo it by purchasing more pairs than you can handle. Start with only four until you have gained some experience. Aim for quality, not quantity.

Selecting Your Budgie

There are a number of considerations which occur to the would-be purchaser of a pet budgerigar: whether to select a male or a female, what color to choose, where to buy your pet, how to tell the age, and how to pick a healthy bird. Under their feathers all budgies are alike. There is no particular advantage of one color over the other in hardiness, intelligence or adaptability.

Color. Choose any color that appeals to your sense of the aesthetic. Opalines, lutinos, fallows, cinnamons, gray-wings, yellow faces, albinos and other seldom seen colors are called "rares." The standard shades of green (light and dark), cobalt, mauve, sky-blue, cobalt white-wings and yellows are called "normals." The rare colors will cost much more than the normals. However, they offer no advantage to the pet owner other than their rarity. If you want an uncommon bird, by all means choose a "rare." If you are selecting a bird entirely for its merits as a pet, select the color that appeals to you.

The Australian dominant pied opaline gray green is represented here by this big bird of good type, color, spots, and head qualities. Perfection is unfortunately not achieved though as this bird's (budgie's) dark tail is considered faulty.

This Australian banded pied yellowface cobalt is exceptionally good in size, color and spots. Notice the distinct band that runs down to the flank. Also characteristic is the patchy rump clearly displayed by this specimen.

This recessive pied mauve is an excellent example of this type of budgie with its good size, type, color and markings. This beautiful bird is a member of a very difficult-to-breed variety of budgerigar.

This dominant Dutch pied olive green shows a similarity to the recessive pieds of this same variety. This attractive bird is not perfect, however, as it lacks back skull and has a drooping tail.

Talking Birds. For many years there was a popular misconception that only male parrakeets would talk, but this has been proved fallacious. Female keets do talk. We have heard many talking female keets with extensive vocabularies. At present there is no such thing as a strain of talkers. If properly taught, almost any keet will learn to talk.

Distinguishing the Sexes. During the period between six weeks and three months of age, the young keet has usually learned caution. It is somewhat wary of humans and will generally try to bite if grabbed suddenly. It is believed that females bite the hardest, and this test is sometimes used in an effort to distinguish the sexes. Another proposed method of sexing six- to twelve-week-old keets, unfortunately unreliable, is by the *cere* or fleshy portion of the beak which surrounds the nostrils. In adult males, the *cere* is bright blue; in adult females it is pink, light blue or brown. In babies—under three months of age—the color of the *cere* is not a reliable indication of the sex, though in males it is apt to be rounder, brighter and stand out more than in females.

Female keets are generally more aggressive than males, more inquisitive, take longer to "get acquainted," are noisier, and take more readily to playing with toys. We consider their antics more amusing.

Young Parrakeets. A keet between the ages of six weeks and three months is young enough to take readily to training. There is considerable risk involved in purchasing a bird under six weeks of age. While baby budgies generally begin eating by themselves between four to five weeks after hatching, their parents (particularly the fathers) continue to feed them until they are six weeks old. It is true that fluffy little five-week-old keets are adorable. They are too young to know fear, and will sit on your finger when placed there. Many persons succumb to the temptation of buying them. But the babies need that extra week of care and feeding to give them a good start toward growing into healthy, strong birds.

The eyes of the baby keet appear much larger than those of the adult. This is because the iris of the baby, like the pupil, is solid black. At about three months of age, the iris begins to grow lighter, and by the time the baby is six months old, its iris has become light gray, although the pupil remains dark for life.

The striations or stripes completely cover the neck and head of a baby budgie. At about ten to twelve weeks of age, these stripes begin to disappear from the forehead, which begins to turn color, white in the case of blue birds and yellow for green and yellow birds. Until six weeks of age the baby also sports a black bill. The black color disappears between six and seven weeks of age.

Selecting Your Bird. In making your choice, select a bird whose feathers are bright, who sits alertly and who responds to movements. Avoid the bird which rests on its elbows, lacks the long tail or wing feathers, seems dull, lethargic or unresponsive. Make sure that the bars on its head extend all the way down to what may be called the nose and that the eyes are solid black. Examine the area around the vent. Discolored yellow feathers usually indicate diarrhea, which is often fatal to young birds.

In the early stages of diarrhea the rump feathers are stained yellow. This color gradually deepens to green and the feathers begin to fall out. The final stages are indicated by a bare rump. The downy white feathers which cover that portion of the anatomy are gone. If something is not done promptly, the bird will die shortly after this latter stage has been reached.

Pick the color you like, but avoid so-called "bargain birds." These are usually defective birds, attractively priced for quick disposal to the unwary purchaser. A pet budgerigar can live twelve or fifteen years and must be considered a long-term investment. A few dollars spent wisely at the beginning will pay dividends in pleasure and enjoyment for many years.

Usually a premium price is asked for hand-raised keets. These are much tamer at the time of purchase than keets which have never been handled. However, any keet under six months of age can be tamed and trained so easily that in a short time it is impossible to distinguish it from one that has been hand-raised.

Whether to buy from a pet shop or a breeder is entirely up to you. Most pet dealers are careful and conscientious, depending on the confidence of their customers for their reputation and continued sales.

This recessive yellow face blue has fairly nice color and markings, but the blue coloring should be more extensive. Another fault of this particular specimen is that its head is too small and lacks back skull.

The recessive pied skyblue pictured here has beautiful color and nice markings. There is no question, though, that its body and head are too small to qualify as an exhibition bird.

This Australian band-
ed pied opaline olive
green is a nice type.
This budgie proudly
displays good color,
correct markings, a
head of the proper
size and shape and
good spots. Every-
thing seems to be
perfect with this bird,
but there is one im-
perfection: the band
is too large; this bird
would never qualify
for competition.

An Australian pied
opaline blue is a nice
big bird of unusual
but striking color.
This particular
specimen lacks a
frontal lift, unfor-
tunately. Its other
fault is that the mask
is too small for its
spots. These faults
would be a deterrent
in competition.

27

Breeding budgerigars has become very popular among fanciers, both outdoors and indoors and one does not have to be an expert to achieve success just as long as certain basic principles are followed.

The Cage and Cage Furnishings

The choice of cage is wide. There is a cage for every purse and every taste. In purchasing a cage for your pet, it is best to avoid one made of wood for there are a number of disadvantages to this kind of cage. Budgies love to gnaw at everything with their strong little beaks and a wooden cage soon will look woebegone and not at all the pretty thing it was when you bought it. Moreover the crevices in the wood offer attractive lodging places for mites.

Chrome which is easy to clean is the best material for a cage. Painted or sprayed cages are often more attractive than the plain chrome, but unless the finish is very hard, the bird will chip off the paint.

A beautiful Australian pied whiteflight cobalt. This budgie is evenly marked. It has good color and type, but careful examination will reveal uneven throat spots which, of course, would be unacceptable in competition.

This Australian pied normal cobalt is a very good size. This bird's type, color and color distribution are satisfactory. Fault can be found, however, in this budgie's band which is slightly small as well as patchy. This bird's crouched stance is not normal, but only an indication that he is frightened.

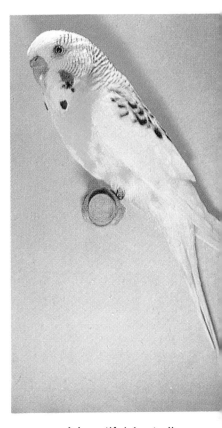

This Australian pied normal dark green has good markings even though they are slightly patchy in color. Its spots are acceptable but the mask is too small. The body and head of this budgie are well-shaped but lacking in size.

A beautiful Australian pied opaline skyblue. This big nicely colored bird appears somewhat too long, the head is lacking in skull, and there are several missing spots.

A cage approximately 9 inches long, 18 inches wide and about 13 inches high is suitable for a single budgie. Too small a cage results in a ragged set of tail feathers and a dirty looking bird. The bars should be set firmly and no wider apart than ½ inch, with a 3/8 inch spacing preferred. The little bird is very strong, and many a pet budgie has forced its way out of a cage made with widely spaced bars. The danger is even greater with flexible bars. A bird may force its head through the center of the cage where the bars provide little resistance to bending, slide down to where the bars are fastened, be unable to get free and strangle itself unless rescued.

There are a number of cages on the market made especially for parrakeets. These have horizontal bars and a wide door opening. However, any large canary cage with close-set bars can be used.

Feeding Cups. The type of feeding cup which sets inside the cage is preferable for keets. If you have a cage with outside cups, place a small dish of water and a dish of seed on the floor of the cage until you are sure that your new pet knows how to use the outside cups. Outside cups are, as the name implies, cups which are fastened to the outside of the cage. An opening in the bars permits the bird to put his head into the cup. As this type of cup is narrower than the square type which fits inside the cage, it is necessary to make sure that it is refilled regularly. Otherwise an accumulation of husks on top could prevent the keet from digging down. This usually takes only a week or two and then you can dispense with the dishes on the floor.

Perches. Perches of different shapes will help rest the bird's feet. It is wise to have extra perches to replace the used ones when you clean the cage. Most birds enjoy a swinging perch.

Never wash the perches. Rough sandpaper or a commercial perch brush can be used to remove all dirt without washing.

Bird Baths. An outside bird bath of the type made for canaries is useful. Many budgies refuse to bathe at first, but when they are persuaded to try it, they love it. If the bird is obstinate about bathing, do not force it. A little gravel on the bottom of the bath will reassure the bird if its reluctance in bathing comes from a fear of slipping. If this does not work, hang an empty bath in place and put seeds in it for a few days instead of in the food cup. Once the bird is used to going in and out of the bath, try it again with just a little water. A little borax or glycerine added to the water will help make the bird's feathers shine.

Cleaning the Cage. The cage floor should have a removable tray for cleaning and a removable bottom to keep the bird from flying out when the tray is removed. Clean your pet's cage once a week. Use a few drops of Lysol in the cleaning water. Sandpaper will clean the perches. Make sure that the cage is thoroughly dry before putting the bird back. A damp cage or damp perches may result in a sick bird, so a little caution will prevent a lot of grief.

Plastic or glass guards around the cage will help prevent seed and gravel from being scattered out of the cage. If these guards are removable, they will be much easier to clean.

Make sure that there are no loose wires, strings, or anything with which the bird could become entangled. Active and inquisitive, a budgie is sure to find them and become tangled, perhaps seriously.

The owner of a recently purchased budgie is quite likely to go overboard in buying cage furnishings. A well-stocked pet shop can display an astonishing number of attractive items, and the temptation to purchase as many as the cage will hold is almost irresistible. But, for the sake of your pet, restraint must be practiced.

There are several "musts" for your bird's health. A cuttle bone is essential. This is the dried shell of the cuttle fish and is almost pure lime. Lime is a form of calcium, one of the minerals most essential to the health of the bird. Test the cuttle bone with your fingernail. The back should be hard and smooth. The face of the cuttle bone should be fairly soft and very dry, scoring easily. Should there be any odor to the bone, reject it as being spoiled. Fasten the cuttle bone securely to the cage bars inside the cage, with the soft part facing in, close to a perch where it can be reached easily. Many people seem to be under the impression that a cuttle bone is used by the bird solely to "sharpen its bill." Actually, the bird is flaking off tiny bits of the bone and eating them. Thus the cuttle bone is a valuable food supplement as well as a help in keeping the beak from growing too long.

A small piece of plaster or a nibble made of two parts of clean river sand to one part slaked lime is also helpful in supplying minerals. Add enough water to make a paste and let it set until hard before giving it to the bird.

For the cage bottom, use a layer of #30 brown gravel, mixed half and half with crushed oyster shell grit, about half an inch deep. (Avoid the white canary gravel.) This should be changed once a week when the cage is cleaned. At one time it was recommended that charcoal be added to this mixture, but recent experiments indicate that charcoal does more harm than good to the budgie.

For ease in cleaning, some owners place a mat of cedarized paper under the gravel to protect the tray. There is no harm in this if the bird does not try to eat the paper. Gravel papers used widely for canaries are not suitable for parrakeets. They do not supply enough grit and the keets will often eat the paper.

Treats. There are many types of treats on the market. Some are made in the form of little cakes which fasten to the bars of the cage. There seems to be no harm in these, and most birds enjoy picking at them. However, they are fattening and should not be used to excess. Large commercial packagers of bird seeds market a product also known as a "treat." Packed in jars, this consists of a mixture of various seeds, often including anise seed which gives the mixture a licorice odor. None of the seeds used in this treat mixture is essential to the bird's health if a balanced diet is being fed. In excess, treat is fattening and therefore should be limited to no more than a level teaspoonful a day. The only reason for feeding treat is that the birds, as said before, seem to enjoy it.

Toys. All kinds of toys for keets to play with are available—a ladder to climb with a bell to ring at the top, a mirror in which the bird admires itself, a seesaw to teeter back and forth, Ferris wheels to ride on, little men called "Kelleys" to play with. "Kelleys" are small figures set on rounded, weighted bases. As the bird knocks them over, they bob back. We have seen a keet play with one for hours.

Toys are available in both wood and plastic. Our personal preference is for the plastic which are easier to clean and less likely to be chewed.

It is best to postpone putting a mirror into the cage until the bird is trained. Forming an attachment for the mirror frequently delays the taming process.

Whatever toys you choose, leave enough room in the cage for the bird. Be extremely careful not to use anything with strings, wires, or small openings into which the keet's head may fit. We cannot repeat often enough that a budgie's curiosity is insatiable. This is at once the bird's greatest charm and most ever-present danger. The bird is afraid of nothing and must investigate everything. Its antics will keep an appreciative audience fascinated for hours on end, but if there is a way of getting into trouble, the parrakeet is sure to find it. It is seldom necessary to teach the bird how to use toys. Just provide them and the little busybody will do the rest.

Some pet shops feature "play pens." These are wooden or chrome trays about 9 by 13 inches, equipped with ladders to climb, bars to swing on, bells to ring and mirrors to chatter into. They are provided with cups for seed and water and, although they are completely open, the little acrobat is usually so busy playing that it just does not care to leave.

Budgerigars are easily trained to do many things, even to ride a car! Just place your bird on a small toy car which is equipped with a little perch and pull the car around the room. Your budgie will enjoy the ride, and you can delight in his pleasure.

It is very important to keep plenty of seeds in the cage at all times. A budgerigar deprived of seeds for twenty-four hours will die. He could also die of starvation if the hulls of the seeds are allowed to accumulate in the seed cup and are mistaken for seeds, so be sure to clean out the hulls every day and replenish the cup with fresh seeds.

Feeding Budgies

The basic diet for the budgerigar in captivity consists of two types of seeds, canary and millet, mixed half and half. For very young budgies, a 60 percent canary and 40 percent millet is even better, since canary seed has a softer shell and is easier for the baby to crack. Should a very young budgie seem to have difficulty cracking the seeds, help the bird by cracking the seeds with a rolling pin before feeding them to the bird. Do not powder them—just break the husk. This is necessary only in the case of a very young bird which you can see is having difficulty in eating. Small amounts of hulled oats and unhulled rice are beneficial additions to the diet.

Seeds. The type of millet preferred for feeding parrakeets is white or proso. This is more nutritious than the yellow millet. Keets have dif-

ficulty in digesting red millet, which is therefore unsuitable as a food for them. The grains of millet should be large, smooth in consistency, and creamy white or light yellow in color. Imported canary seed is preferable, and these seeds should be plump, shiny and smooth.

Millet sprays, that is, sprays out of which the millet seeds have not been thrashed, are sold by many pet shops. Keets seem to enjoy climbing over these sprays and picking out the seeds.

Greens. Greens should be fed once a day. All dark green vegetables contain minerals and vitamins essential to the bird's health. A partial list of greens would include dandelion, carrot greens and grated carrot, broccoli, kale, dark green or romaine lettuce, and chickweed.

Feed as much as the bird will eat of the greens in an hour or two. Failure to provide greens regularly may cause the bird to overindulge when the greens are fed. This may result in the parrakeet getting diarrhea. The best cure for this is prevention. If your pet has not had greens for some time, give them sparingly until the bird is used to them.

Many pet budgies, when first fed greens, do not attempt to try them. If your budgie does not eat the greens when they are given, soak them in water for a few minutes and then feed them to the bird. At the same time remove the water cup. It rarely takes more than a lesson or two to get the parrakeet started eating the greens. Should your bird be especially stubborn, remove the water cup two hours before giving the greens and allow the moist greens to remain in the cage with no other water available. Repeat this if necessary. Once a keet has tasted greens, the bird will take to them readily.

A commercially available clip or even a paper clip can be used to fasten the greens in place. Never allow the greens to lie on the floor of the cage where they will be dirtied. Then too, hanging the greens makes them approximate an ornament and encourages the bird to play with and bite at them.

Make sure that all greens are fresh, clean and very carefully washed to remove any bug spray or poison. It is better to skip a meal of greens than to feed wilted ones. Whenever possible use the young, succulent leaves.

Other Foods. A little egg yolk crumbled with an equal amount of cracker crumbs and moistened slightly makes a nutritious treat, as does a weekly feeding of bread and milk.

Raw egg contains a vitamin D destroying factor. All egg fed to a keet must be boiled for at least 20 minutes. This boiling destroys the B-inhibiting enzyme, while retaining most of the essential nutritional value. These last two meals are particularly valuable for budgies that are not in the best of health. In feeding bread and milk to a sick budgie, it is best to bring the milk to a boil and then cool it before offering it to the bird. Soaked seeds are quite beneficial to babies and breeders.

A tame budgie soon learns to sit at the table and eat foods from its owner's plate. While this is very cute, it is not always best for the bird. When a bird comes in contact with unfamiliar food, its instinct cannot be depended upon to select what is good for it. You must watch and see that the bird does not eat starchy, spicy or greasy fried foods.

Vitamins. In a natural state the ultra violet rays of the sun act on the ergosterol in a bird's feathers to produce vitamin D. However, glass filters out the violet rays of the sun and for that reason it is necessary to use cod-liver oil as a vitamin supplement for budgies that are kept indoors. Add 8 drops of cod-liver oil to each pound of seeds. As both vitamins A and D are apt to lose their strength when standing exposed to the air, it is best to add a proportionate amount of fresh oil to the seed each week or better still fortify only a week's supply at one time.

The further addition of a small pinch of brewer's yeast (available in any drug store) to the seed cup every other day will insure an adequate supply of the B vitamins.

Digestive Disorders. One of the first indications of upset digestion or of poor health in budgies is the changed appearance of the droppings. The feces of a healthy budgie are semi-solid with a light center and a dark green edge. Should the droppings become watery or change in consistency, it is advisable to check the diet carefully for signs of spoiled food. Discard anything which shows signs of mold. Discontinue greens temporarily, boil the drinking water and feed boiled milk and bread.

A Good Diet and a Healthy Bird. Food should be available at all times to the budgerigar, since these small birds succumb quickly to starvation. The budgie is, by nature, a very healthy bird. If it is given all the seed it wants, enough fresh greens, occasionally a serving of egg yolk, bread and milk, a good grit, a cuttle bone and cod-liver oil, you need have no worries about the parrakeet's diet.

A tame single budgie, whether a talker or not and whether a male or female, enjoys inventing his own tricks.

First Steps in Training

For proper training the location of the cage is of particular importance and a place should be selected before the bird is brought home. Although budgies are tolerant of extremes in temperatures, they cannot tolerate drafts. A light, draft-free location about five feet off the floor is ideal. The cage may have a stand, bracket, or even be placed on a shelf.

A kitchen had best be avoided as a site for a budgie cage, unless it is large and airy. The frequent and extreme changes of temperature due to cooking can work havoc with a keet. Another factor to be considered is a bird's extreme sensitivity to gas. At one time birds were used extensively in mines as gas detectors. The birds would give warning by passing out at the first whiff of gas, long before a man could even detect an odor.

Avoid placing the cage in direct sunlight. A budgie confined in a cage that is in direct sunlight is in great danger, even in the relatively mild sunlight of a winter's day. Do not go to the other extreme and keep your bird at very low temperatures. While it is true that many commercial breeders keep their birds outdoors all winter, it must be remembered that exercising in long flights helps to keep them warm, and at night they conserve body heat by huddling together.

Wing Clipping. Many authorities advocate clipping the wing feathers before taming. We are opposed to this practice which we feel is unnecessary and unfair to the bird. Compare the swift, free, graceful flight of an unclipped budgie with the awkward, fearful attempts made by one with clipped wings. As the poor bird tries to fly and realizes that it cannot control its flight, it becomes timid and unsure of itself. The whole personality of the bird is thwarted and it becomes a poor pet. Unscrupulous dealers have been known to clip wings of older budgies and sell them as "finger tamed" at a higher price, when actually the poor bird was only clinging to the finger for fear of falling.

In our opinion, the only valid excuse for clipping a budgie's wings would be to make it a "trick bird." A budgie with clipped wings can be taught tricks more readily since it cannot fly away from the trainer. These birds are not generally allowed their freedom but are confined at all times except when taken out for lessons.

A pet budgie will teach itself many cute little tricks or learn them with a little encouragement from you. We have finger trained hundreds of parrakeets and have never found that it was necessary to clip the wings of one. We have taken keets given up as incorrigible by their owners, and in a short time—a few days to a few weeks—have finger tamed the worst of them without a feather falling before the onslaught of a scissors.

Finger and Tee Stick Training. When the trip home from the place of purchase is not too long, it is best to start finger training about half an hour after placing the bird in the cage. Should the trip take longer or involve shipping, the new owner should wait overnight. It is a mistake to wait any longer than this. A young bird is lonely and frightened at first in its new home. In almost every case, it has spent its short life in the company of its own kind. It is by filling that need for companionship that you attach the bird's affections to you. Too long a delay at the beginning may mean that, to the parrakeet, you become simply a part of the surroundings.

Leaving the bird alone or moving away from the cage when your parrakeet flutters is the worst thing you can do. A bird learns by association of ideas. Should you move away whenever you budgie flutters in fright, it soon will learn to associate fluttering with your withdrawal and then begin to feel that actually you have been chased away. This, of course, makes things much more difficult when the actual training begins.

A young budgie in strange surroundings is generally inclined to be quiet and inactive for the first few weeks. As long as the bird does not show any disease symptoms, you need not be concerned. The parrakeet will be active enough when it becomes more familiar with the new environment. Due to nervousness, the droppings of the newly acquired bird tend to be softer than normal. This condition, however, should not persist for longer than a few days.

Often a baby keet is so frightened for the first few days that it will not eat when any one is near. This frequently leads to people calling us up to say, "My keet hasn't eaten since I brought him home. What shall I do?" The best thing to do is to check the seeds carefully for the husks which are the best evidence that he has been eating. The little fellow has been sneaking down to eat when no one is around and scuttling back to a perch so soon as he hears footsteps.

Start your pet's training by slowly putting your finger into the cage. Talk gently to the bird. It does not matter what you say (reciting nursery rhymes will do), but it is essential that the sound of your voice be associated with you. Later this will be a great help in teaching the parrakeet to talk.

Slowly move your finger so as to stroke the breast of the bird. Then, moving extremely slowly, place your forefinger under its chest, just in front of the place where the legs join the body. By gently lifting, the parrakeet will step up on your finger to regain its balance. Hold your finger very still and keep talking all the time. After a few minutes, move your hand slowly so that one of the perches presses against the bird's chest. The keet will then step up on the perch, and you will have successfully completed your first lesson.

Do not be discouraged if the bird flutters wildly and, above all, do not jerk your hand away suddenly. Keep still until the budgie quiets down, and then, still talking gently, approach it again with your finger. Try to avoid moving your hand over its head. All birds have an instinctive fear of objects approaching from above—this is probably a hereditary fear of hawks. When you do find it necessary to approach from above, do it slowly and deliberately so that the bird can see what you are doing without being startled.

As long as the bird moves away from your finger, continue to follow it. As the budgie brushes by your finger or even jumps on it looking around for a way to escape, it will gradually come to realize that no harm is meant and that, in fact, your finger is nice and warm and much more comfortable to sit on than one of the hard wooden perches.

Confine your lessons to a fifteen-minute period, four or five times daily. Always try to leave the lesson at a successful moment, that is, just after you have held the bird on your finger. Should this be impossible, at least stroke your pet several times before withdrawing your hand. As we have said before, do not leave the bird feeling that it has driven you away.

Often a bird that sits docilely on your finger at the end of a lesson has become quite wild by the time you begin your next lesson. It may have been frightened by something in the interval, or it may have just forgotten you, but in any case, this is nothing about which to be concerned. Ignore your budgie's wildness and your pet will soon calm down.

Many birds are naturally good-natured and take very readily to training. Others have a more uncooperative nature and require time and special attention. Budgie personalities vary with the individual birds. A budgie will also react to the kind of treatment it receives. If you are gentle from the beginning you will have a gentle bird, if you are rough or teasing, your budgie may develop into a noisy, biting, disobedient pet.

Some people prefer to start training by using a tee stick (two round half-inch dowell sticks fastened in the form of the letter T, the head of which is six inches long and the handle about two feet). The procedure for training with a tee stick is the same as for hand training except that the head of the tee stick is substituted for your finger. Pass the tee stick slowly through the door or bars of the cage and press it against the bird's breast until it forces the bird to step on the wood. The advantage of the tee stick training is that it will enable you to reach up to the bird when it has its freedom and perches in high places. When your parrakeet has learned to accept the tee stick in the cage, you can start finger taming.

Whether you use the finger, the stick, or both, select a command to be given when lifting the bird. Whatever word you use, be sure that it is short, clear, and that you repeat it every time you pick up the bird. We use the command "up" coupled with the bird's name. This serves a double purpose; the bird soon learns its name and is conditioned to accept commands. We have found this conditioning most useful in advanced training.

Avoid uncaging the bird until it gets on your finger readily on command. The best time for taking your pet from the cage is in the evening, for during the day the parrakeet may try to fly out of a window through which the light enters, whereas a dark window offers no attraction. It is also much easier to recapture the bird in the evening, should that be necessary.

Open the door of the cage and hook it—a small piece of bent wire will serve if there is no catch. Place the bird on your finger with the command "up." Slowly withdraw your hand from the cage and walk around the room, talking soothing chatter to the bird all the time, with many repetitions of its name. After a few minutes place your pet back in the cage and close the door.

Sooner or later your budgie will become emboldened by familiarity or perhaps be startled by something, and will fly off your finger. Do not try to catch the bird, but remain still until it alights. Then move slowly toward it with your finger outstretched and give the command "up" once again. If the lessons have been taught well, the parrakeet will step up on your finger and may be returned to the cage. Should your pet be over-exhilarated by freedom and fly away, do not grab for the bird, but wait until it alights and try again. If all efforts fail, mark the position where the bird lands and have a helper turn off the lights—a bird will not try to fly in the dark. It may then be picked up easily and returned to its cage. If, by chance, your keet should escape during the day, it can be caught by dropping a towel over it and picking both towel and bird gently from its resting place.

Continue to stroke your pet during all its lessons. You will find that it enjoys having its head and throat scratched. In a short time it will allow you to pick it up in order to get its head scratched.

Biting is a vice found in very few budgies. It is used only as a means of defense by a terrified bird. A budgie rarely attempts to bite while being finger tamed. The only time it may attempt this is when being grasped too suddenly. In its struggles to get free, it may resort to biting. Should this happen, tap the bird on the beak to make it release its hold.

It is important to hold a keet correctly so as to restrain its struggles without injuring it. The back of the bird is held in the palm of the hand, the thumb and forefinger form a ring around its neck to keep the bird from pushing forward, and the little finger forms a ring around the tail to prevent the bird from pulling back. The third and fourth fingers confine the body and legs. Hold the bird in this manner and scratch its head until the budgie relaxes. Practice this many times until the bird will turn over in your hand on the word of command and with just a little pressure from your finger. By continuing this training you can get the keet to roll over and lie on its back on a toy bed or a small wagon.

Training budgies to do formal tricks on command requires a great deal of time and patience. As we have said before, in our opinion "trick bird" training is the only valid excuse for wing clipping. This prevents the bird's flying away when tiring of a lesson. The use of a long stick, similar to a classroom pointer, makes it easier to control the bird. Notch

This young bird has the right type, color, spot and head qualities that make him an excellent candidate for breeding purposes. It would be a pity to train this type of bird, because trained birds do not breed as well as those that are not.

the stick so that the bird can cling to it. With the bird on one end, slowly lower the stick and, as the bird climbs, give the command "climb." Encourage your pet to reach the top and then reverse the pitch so that it can continue to make the bird climb. After a while, your keet will climb a rope, curtain or small ladder in response to the simple command.

Budgie in Wagon. A trick that can be taught with very little difficulty is to ride in a small wagon. Allow the bird to become accustomed to the wagon by rolling it back and forth in front of your pet as it perches on its training stick. Then place the bird in the wagon and slowly pull it back and forth giving the command "ride." Do not make the lesson too long at first. Most budgies enjoy riding around and will soon ride almost anything in response to the command.

There are many other tricks which, with a little ingenuity and patience, can be taught to a budgie. For the more ambitious there is the possibility of a whole budgie circus. The time required for this undertaking is far more than the average reader of this book is prepared to spend.

Some of the more difficult tricks may take a year or more to teach to the bird. We have included a few tricks to show the possibilities of training. Since this book is concerned primarily with pet budgies in the home, we do not feel it necessary to go into greater detail on trick training. Our feeling is that the rigorous training and discipline necessary to training a "trick" bird in large measure spoils it for a pet. To us, the greatest fascination of these birds is their charming lack of discipline.

In a home they will constantly entertain you with the tricks they teach themselves. Each one will be a fresh surprise to you, and your bird an endless source of delight. So just sit back and relax. Let the bird take the center of the stage. Finger tame your pet, teach it to fly to and from its cage, and leave it to its own accord. Call it by name whenever you feed your pet or give it tidbits. It will soon fly to you and perch on your shoulder or outstretched finger.

A frequently voiced problem is "My tame parrakeet sits on my shoulders and if I don't play with him he bites my neck or cheek." Without realizing it, you yourself have taught your pet to do this. A pet parrakeet sitting on its owner's shoulder nibbles on everything within reach, clothing, jewelry, and flesh. Should he accidently nip, the immediate reaction is to pick him up and hold him to your face for a scolding. This he finds delightful. It doesn't take long before he realizes that a bite will always bring this result. The remedy is to nip the nipper in the bud. As soon as he bites flick him off his perch. Use a towel or cloth in preference to a hand. A few salutary lessons of this sort and he will stop biting. But you must be consistent and punish him every time.

Only a bird that is kept alone and away from other birds will learn to do tricks and talk and become an affectionate pet.

Teaching a Budgie to Talk

Training your pet to talk is very easily accomplished. It will soon learn to know your voice if you talk to it while you are feeding it. After a few weeks you will notice that it lifts its head and stops to listen when you speak. This is the time to start speech training. Select a short, easy word or phrase. Never try to teach a partial phrase, intending to teach the rest later. It just will not work that way. The bird will not be able to connect the two parts of the phrase and, unless each half alone makes sense, the result will be gibberish. You must remember that a bird does not speak in the same sense that we do. It is merely imitating sounds. The words themselves have no meaning to your pet. By the same token, the budgie will imitate many other sounds it hears—the creak of a door, the whir of a machine, or the often-heard song of a canary. In the case of one bird kept in a poolroom, it was the whir of the balls and the clack as they struck that it imitated.

Another thing to bear in mind is that a budgie has no discrimination in what it repeats. It will repeat the sound regardless of its owners' wishes, and is unable to judge the appropriateness of the words.

Mid-morning and early evening are the best time for speech training. Although many birds pick up words from various members of the family, it is best to reserve the training to only one person. Confine the bird to its cage for a short time before, during and after its lesson. Stand to one side where your pet cannot see you but can hear you distinctly. In a clear voice repeat the phrase selected. Speak slowly and pause between each repetition. This should be done for ten minutes at a time, twice a day. The bird will recognize your voice. It may even press against the bars of the cage in an effort to get to you. One fine day you will find your pet sitting quietly on a perch mumbling to itself. This is your pet's method of practicing, and before too long you will hear the lesson being repeated. Be sure that a lesson is known perfectly before going on to the next one. To the question, "how long before my bird will talk?" We can only answer, "We don't know." We have known several birds which said their first words before they were three months of age. We should say six months of age is about average, but do not be too discouraged if it takes longer. We sold one bird we were unable to teach to talk at six months of age. It did not say a word until it was a year old, and in the six months after learning its first word, it learned one hundred and fifty more.

We have compared the length of time required for speech training, utilizing different methods, and have found this one to be the shortest. Several keets which their owners trained under our instructions were talking by three months of age.

Much, of course, depends on your teaching. There are several things to bear in mind. Try to train at a time when distracting noises are at a minimum. Always have the same person do the training. Do not change the instructor or the phrase until it is fully learned, regardless of the time involved. A parakeet's voice is small, and it has a tendency to speak faster than we do and run the words together. Therefore, it is important that you speak more slowly than you would normally, enunciating each word clearly and pausing for a few seconds at the end of each word.

Special phonograph records can be purchased for use in speech training. These are helpful for the owner who has little time to spare or insufficient patience. Records of a budgie speaking are also available but none of those that we have heard have been really distinct. Add to an indistinct record a budgie's normal tendency to garble words and the result is not likely to be the one desired.

You should also take into consideration the fact that a budgie not only mimics your words but also your manner of speaking them. This, of course, means that if it mimics a record, it will be imitating a stranger, and the charming intimacy of having your own bird repeating your own speech is lost.

Some people advocate holding a budgie on a finger close to one's lips while training it to talk. In our opinion this method offers several disadvantages. A bird will not learn to speak by watching your lips. Its words are formed in its throat and lip movement has no part in it. The motion of your lips is more of a distraction than a help. The reason your budgie watches your lips so intently is that the bird has a normal curiosity in any moving object. It is very difficult to make an active budgie sit still on your finger for ten minutes at a time. Long before the lesson is over, it is likely to fly off and ignore you. And, needless to say, it is also hard for you to remain still for the duration of the lesson. Any moves you make while the bird is sitting on your finger serve to take its mind away from what you are trying to teach to it.

This is not to say that the method we advocate is the only method of speech training. As a matter of fact, many birds have picked up words without any formal training. We do feel, however, that the method we have outlined, if it is followed carefully, will bring the best results in the shortest time.

The first few phrases are the hardest. The more the bird learns, the easier the training becomes, and while the first word may take six months, the next should take only as many weeks. Once a budgie becomes adept at imitating, it can learn a simple phrase in a few days.

Singing and whistling a tune are taught the same way as speaking—through repetition. It is best to avoid teaching whistling until the bird is an accomplished talker. Whistling is much easier for the bird to learn, and it may not pay attention to the spoken word once it has learned to whistle.

It is not at all unusual for a pet budgie kept alone to sit in front of a mirror and talk to it. During this conversation, the bird may regurgitate food once or even a number of times. This is perfectly normal. Budgerigar parents feed their babies with food which they regurgitate from their crops. Your pet budgie is just trying to be friendly and feed the image in the mirror.

A budgie is usually most satisfactory as a pet when kept alone. It is very difficult to train two budgies kept together, and almost impossible to teach them to talk when they have the company of their own kind. The person who wants to have more than one budgie should keep the individuals out of sight and hearing of each other until they are trained, when they may be placed together.

There is not much wrong with this beautiful green cock!

Yellow wing light
green cock.

Another method is to have one bird fully trained before placing a new one with it. If your training has been well assimilated, your pet will remain tame. On the other hand, if your training has not been thorough enough, your pet budgie may become quite wild, preferring the company of the other bird to that of yours.

A young bird placed with a good talker may learn to talk by imitation. This, however, is the exception rather than the rule, and it is quite possible that the trained bird may imitate the bird chatter of the new arrival and forget all about talking.

One budgie we know had been kept alone by its owners for more than a year. One day its master decided that it needed company and brought a baby bird home to share the pet's cage. To say that the pet budgie was astounded would be putting it mildly. It had often talked to the budgie in the mirror, but this was the first time that a budgie was there to talk back. When the baby tried to cuddle up, the older bird was terrified and fled screeching from the intruder. Released from its cage, the pet bird flew wildly around the room and refused to allow its beloved owner to approach. In order to preserve the pet's sanity, the new bird had to be removed. In a few days, all was forgiven and the pet again became a loveable, charming companion.

It is this loss of all its wild instincts which makes a pet budgie unsuitable for breeding. He, or she, as the case may be, just does not seem to know how to go about it. In many cases they are unable to complete the matings. When eggs are laid, they are in doubt as to how to incubate them, and as for feeding youngsters . . . horrors! Even when the mate which has been procured for the pet budgie is a proven breeder, there is usually trouble. It eventually becomes disgusted with its uncooperative spouse and winds up thrashing it, to the detriment of eggs or young.

This is one of the reasons why it is so difficult to build up a strain of talking budgerigars. The only way to prove a bird capable of talking is by training it. Once it is trained, it is rarely any good for breeding. Should it breed, the same process must be gone through with the youngsters and continued for a number of generations before any definite results can be hoped for. All these potential talkers must be isolated from all other keets and even from each other in order to teach them to speak. Once the talkers are selected, they must be bred, with odds against it being successful. The difficulties are almost insurmountable, and it is doubtful that the results would justify the effort.

The following account of taming of parrakeets in India we found particularly interesting. The birds used are not our own little budgerigars. However, there is no doubt but that the account would remain substantially the same if budgies were substituted. The training methods used and the tricks taught are well within the scope of learning of our own budgerigar. Actually many of the tricks mentioned in this account have been taught to keets by trainers working independently over here. We have no doubt but that the methods used are essentially the same.

THE TAMING OF PARROTS IN BARODA

From the Bulletin of the Baroda State Museum and Picture Gallery.

"The tricks are indeed amazing which the long-tailed Parrakeets, popularly known as the Parrots, have in Baroda been tamed and trained in. To win confidence of naturally shy birds, no little tact is required. Great credit must, therefore, be given to the keeper of the Baroda parrot show. For, unacquainted with modern methods of bird-keeping, he seldom fails in his attempts to bring up the birds under his care. His lack of scientific knowledge, however is balanced by a loving heart, patient care, and the wisdom of traditional experience.

"At times he works wonders with his primitive methods and his proteges are often as tame as a cat or a dog. . .

"The most common kind in Gujerat is the Rose-ring parrakeet (*Psittacula krameri* Scop) called Suda in vernacular. Nearly three-fourths of the trained birds belong to the species.

"It is very affectionate and confiding and its tender attachment to its master makes it a great pet and apt pupil. The young ones are generally chosen for the purpose of training when four to six months old; then their memory is considered to be fairly good and their character altogether more intelligent and docile. A parrot under four months is considered too young to be trained. Their acrobatic capacities are generally attributed to the climbing strength of the feet which possess two toes in front and two behind, and to their mobile beak likewise used for the same purpose. But above all is their intelligence undoubtedly superior to that of any other kind of bird.

"Before the training is begun, the wings (premarcis) of the young ones are cut about an inch or so to avoid their possible escape into the jungle. They are then made to feel quite at home with the trainer and his surroundings. Every evening they are taken round through the noise and rattle of the city perched on a finger or shoulder in order to make them bold and without fear of man and his activities. Both the male and female birds can be taught with the same facility, but it needs the utmost gentleness of expression and caress to teach them the running of a toy cycle or motor car.

"In the beginning they show bad temper and bite, but once they get accustomed to their daily routine business they are very active and hop about nimbly in their eagerness to do the various tricks they have to learn.

"The trainer repeats the words of instruction almost continuously before the young parrot and helps it in the performance of its task. Though, of course, every concession to the mood and temperament of the bird must be made at the moment, utmost patience is exercised to induce it to do its work.

"After a month or two, varying according to the individual capacity of the birds, they learn to listen, understand and execute the performance in obedience to the instructions of their trainer. However the daily lesson does not last for more than 20 minutes. If this time is exceeded the bird becomes irritated and tries to run away. Overtaxed birds not seldom get brain fever and ultimately become useless for any work. The trainer therefore maintains 8 or 10 of his pets in order to avoid any undue strain on a particular bird, and each one is trained only in the one or two numbers of the programme of the parrot show. The programme consists of quite an interesting (variety) of performances such as shooting arrows, hoisting the state flag, driving a motor car, firing a toy gun, and so on. The most interesting item on the programme, however, is a motor car accident where a parrot cycling across a road is struck by a motor car driven by another parrot. The injured parrot feigns to be in a serious condition and lies still on the road side. In the meanwhile the driver runs to the neighboring telephone and sends an urgent call to the doctor. Soon, a third parrot arrives on the scene with his stethoscope, examines the patient and administers some drug out of a phial from the First Aid Box. The patient recovers his senses and then the cyclist, the motor driver and the doctor go their respective ways, and the show is over amidst the great amusement of the spectators.

"After the end of each number the birds are patted and treated in the most friendly and affectionate manner and respond with repeated excited screaming. The least period required by a young parrot for attaining perfection in this performance is six months."

A playground affords a means of keeping
a budgie happily occupied.

Regardless of whether you want a tamed bird or one to use for the purpose of breeding, there are certain rules that must be followed in order to obtain success. Hygienic conditions in the birdroom are an absolute must.

General Suggestions for Keeping Budgies

There are a number of questions which the new owner of a budgie invariably asks.

The neat housewife is naturally concerned about her drapes and covers when told that a budgie flies freely around the house. This paragraph is written to allay that concern. The droppings of a budgie are relatively firm. When allowed to dry, they can be brushed up with a whisk broom without leaving a stain.

Another question often asked is, "How hardy is a keet and how long will it live?" We have no hesitation in saying that the budgerigar is the hardiest of all the small cage birds. With a minimum of care, a pet parakeet can live from ten to twelve years. There are records of their reaching the ripe age of twenty in captivity, and fifteen is not uncommon.

Still another question is, "How do I keep my bird clean?" The budgie normally requires no cleaning. It constantly preens its feathers and with its strong little bill removes every vestige of dirt. Occasionally, however, a budgie flying free around the house gets into something which it cannot clean off. At such a time, a bath is in order. Prepare two bowls of warm water and add a little detergent to one. Holding the budgie gently but firmly, immerse the bird in the water containing the detergent. Make sure that its head is not submerged. With a soft brush, work the lather in well. Holding the bird's wings open against the side of the bowl, clean them well. A soft sponge can be used to clean its head with the greatest possible gentleness. Be careful of the nostrils and eyes. With this accomplished, rinse the bird well in the bowl of clear water. To dry, wrap the budgie carefully in a soft cloth and place the bird in a warm place. Always rub in the direction in which the feathers grow. Needless to say, make sure that the room is warm both during and after the bath.

New owners want to know the reasons for feather loss. There are, as a matter of fact, several causes. Molting in birds is controlled to a great extent by the number of daylight hours and to some extent by the temperature. Normally, a bird's spring molt begins in February and the fall molt in August. On the average, the bird's molt will take about six weeks. However, with the artificial light and the temperature of our homes, a budgie may molt all year round or at any time during the year.

The first or so-called "baby molt" takes place when the bird is about three months of age, regardless of the time of year. It is at this time that it loses the baby stripes on the forehead and that the pretty patches on the cheeks and the necklace on the throat appear.

At no time should a molt cause a bird to have bare spots. If these should appear, they may be due to any one or a combination of a number of things. Mites are one of the worst offenders. There are several types and all of them are undesirable. Many are large enough to be seen with the naked eye, although a magnifying glass will aid in detecting them. They can usually be found in cracks or crevices of the cage. Mites usually do their nefarious blood sucking at night, leaving the bird during the day. One effective way of detecting certain types of mites is to cover the cage at night with a white flannel cloth. In the morning, upon careful examination the mites will be seen as red pinhead size spots on the cloth.

A bird has two oil glands situated at the base of the tail. It will reach back to these glands then run its bill over its feathers. This is known as preening and is perfectly normal. Should the bird scratch excessively or make sudden sharp jabs at itself, it is probably being distressed by mites.

There are several commercial sprays on the market which are effective in controlling mites. Be sure to read the directions and follow them carefully, as the sprays may be toxic if not properly used. It is also advisable to recheck the diet at the same time. Have you been feeding greens regularly? Have you given your bird a good grade of grit? Is the cuttle bone fresh?

Another not uncommon cause of feather loss is a damp, moist atmosphere. The cage may be hung too near a radiator during the winter, and as a result, the bird is forced to live in a steam bath. Hanging the cage too near an outside wall may have the same effect. During the warm months, the sun shining on the outside wall may heat it enough to cause suffering to the bird confined close to the inside wall.

Do not forget to cover your pet's cage in the evening. A baby budgie requires plenty of rest. In nature, a bird goes to sleep with the sun, and in the home it is best to cover the cage before eight o'clock. An older bird, like an older child, may be permitted later hours within reason.

Do not be surprised, on uncovering the cage in the morning or during the night, to find that your pet budgie has slept clinging to the wire bars. This is a very common practice with some birds. The muscles in a bird's feet lock automatically when grasping or clinging so that it can sleep balanced on a perch or clinging to the bars without danger of falling. Some baby budgies even cling to the bars all night with their bills as well as with their feet. This does them no harm. Leave them alone and they will soon start using the perches for sleeping.

A pet budgie loves to ride around the house on its master's shoulder. It sits there so quietly the owner is apt to forget its presence and walk out of the house. A pet budgie, suddenly released in the open, usually becomes confused. Strong, swift fliers, once they have their freedom they are capable of flying a great distance from their home before they land, tired out.

If you can possibly keep track of the flight, you may be able to approach and recover your pet once the initial surge of wildness has passed off. However, in a wooded area or where there are many buildings, this is very difficult to do and your pet may be irretrievably lost. Eventually it will tire of its freedom and try to find its way back, but that is rarely possible. A bird escaping for the first time may fly into a strange window or approach a strange person with all the confidence in the world. For this reason, if no other, it is most inadvisable to try to teach a budgie to go in and out of a house. They are nomadic by nature

and tend to wander. Being curious and trusting, the bird may easily fall into the wrong hands and end up a lost bird.

On an estate in England, "homing budgies" are kept. These birds are trained to return to the aviaries, much as pigeons are trained to return to the loft. However, keets in a flock are different from one keet by itself. They are gregarious and one follows the other. There is much less tendency to stray on the part of the individual when there is a flock to stay with. Even so, the owner of this English flock does admit to regular losses.

Again, as with so many other things, prevention is certainly the best cure. If you wish to keep your pet, my advice is to see that it does not get out of the house. Should you make the mistake of walking out of the house with your budgie on your shoulder, do not startle the bird by making any sudden movement. If you are close to the door, try to step back in or, that failing, see if the bird will step on your finger. When it does that, capture it by putting your thumb on its toes and do not let go.

Below and opposite: Budgies are, in general, very healthy and vigorous birds, and only a small percentage of them actually get sick. Still, besides having a hospital cage that can maintain an even temperature, day and night, of 70°F., fanciers should keep some medicines and preventives as well as supplements on hand.

The budgies at left are about sixteen days old. Prior to mating, a pair of budgies (below) show their readiness for breeding by feeding one another.

Breeding

It is natural for the owner of a pet budgie to consider breeding. There is a little of the "matchmaker" in each of us, and what better subject would there be on which to exercise this inclination than the charming bundle of fluff flitting around the living room. Unfortunately, the *pet* budgie is not ideal for breeding purposes. The very fact of its having been tamed has caused the bird to lose its wild instincts. Presented with a mate, the pet budgie does not know what to do with the female; when the eggs are laid, the pet does not know how to incubate them; when the young come, the poor bewildered pet does not know how to feed them.

One pet keet named Pedro was presented by its adoring mistress with a female which had been raised in an aviary. Confined to its cage, Pedro sulked for a time, but finally nature asserted itself and the pair set about housekeeping. In spite of Pedro's ineptitude, things went along well enough until the babies came. Pedro decided that those squalling brats were no children of his and that he wasn't going to have anything to do with them. For a few days, the female seemed tolerant of the situation. She would leave the nest to sit next to Pedro and preen the feathers around his neck while appearing to whisper sweet nothings in his ear. Despairing of conversation, she would nudge him gently toward the nest, but Pedro would have none of that. One day her patience broke down and, with a fearful screech, she attacked her erring spouse. Only the owner's intervention and the immediate removal of Pedro from the cage prevented murder. The story has a happy ending—once her husband was removed, she settled down and raised the five healthy, charming youngsters by herself. She and her brood were given to a commercial breeder who appreciated her talents as a mother. As for Pedro, so far as We know, he is still the most lovable of pets, flying freely around the house, talking to visitors, with not a tear or regret for his long gone spouse.

The solution for the pet budgie owner who wants to breed is quite simple. Keep your pet as a pet, and acquire a pair or more of adult parrakeets for breeding. The presence of a pet budgie flying around will rarely disturb the breeders, and if they are provided with the proper facilities, they will start mating immediately.

We cannot stress strongly enough the benefit to children of breeding budgerigars. Both male and female are devoted and exemplary parents, the female incubating the eggs while the male feeds her, and both feeding the young.

What better way is there to teach your children the facts of life than by breeding birds? The knowledge acquired this way is taken for granted and inevitably helps develop a much more balanced outlook on life than similar knowledge come upon in a less matter-of-fact and natural fashion. Why lecture on wild birds and bees when having birds in your home is so much more effective?

Breeding in Captivity. In captivity, budgies breed very readily. So readily, in fact, that there may be a tendency to over-breed them. Raising a large nest of birds is quite a strain on the parents, and they should be rested at regular intervals. Two clutches, of four or five young each, are considered the usual number. In nature, birds have fixed mating seasons. These usually coincide with the periods of the greatest abundance of food, so as to insure adequate nutrition of the youngsters.

Under the artificial conditions of the home, breeding can, and often does, take place at any time of the year. However, most authorities recommend that breeding begin shortly before Christmas, the pairs being placed together about the middle of December, that two consecutive nests be raised, and that the parents then be allowed to rest for the balance of the year. When breeding outdoors, it is best to defer all breeding activity until May when the weather is settled.

Ending the Breeding Season. There are two methods for ending the breeding season. The simplest way for owners with limited facilities is to remove all eggs laid after the second clutch has hatched and then, when the babies leave the nest, remove the nest box. A budgie will rarely breed without a suitable nest box.

The second method is to separate the sexes from each other at the end of each breeding season. All the birds of one sex may be kept together. Contrary to popular belief, the parrakeet is not strictly monogamous. While the male has a chosen mate with whom he pairs when breeding, he is not above a little light dalliance on the side. Pairs can be broken up and re-mated. When doing this, it is best to keep them away from their original mates, at least until the first eggs are laid.

Controlled Breeding. Breeding operations may be classified as controlled and aviary or colony breeding. In controlled breeding, pairs are kept in individual cages. This insures that the bird keeps to the mate you have chosen for the male, and thus removes doubts as to the paternity of the youngsters. Controlled breeding is the method best suited to the home breeder. A person can breed as few or as many pairs as wanted. A sun porch, an unused room, a converted attic, or even a bedroom can all be used successfully as a place for breeding parrakeets. A southern exposure is preferable and cleanliness is essential.

For the home breeder, a cage about 3 feet long, 18 inches by 18 inches will give the best results. Not too many perches should be used, so that space is left for flight exercise. All perches should be set firmly in place and slightly roughened to insure a firm grip for the bird. Do not use swinging perches in the breeding cage.

The Mechanics of Breeding. Budgies in good condition and ready for mating have hard glossy feathers, bright eyes and are alert and active. The cere of the male will be bright blue with a bright sheen. He will approach the female with his head bobbing and the pupils of his eyes will contract and expand with the ardor of his emotions. The cere of the female becomes nut brown and corrugated in appearance. She responds alertly to the male's attentions and is very restless.

Budgie mating is preceded by much love making, feather preening and kissing. The actual mating is accomplished by the male's mounting the female. Balancing himself with his wings, the male swings his tail under that of the female so that their cloacas touch. It is at this time that the male sperm is extruded to fertilize the female egg. In birds, the excretory and the sex organs all end at one opening which is called the *cloaca*. It is also through this opening that the eggs are laid. Eggs can be expected in eight to ten days after the actual mating. Smooth or unsteady perches often result in incomplete matings and infertile eggs.

At one end of the cage a nest box approximately 8½ inches high and 5½ to 6 inches square is hung outside the cage, with the round opening of approximately 1½ inches in diameter against a corresponding opening in the end of the cage. A small 3/8 inch diameter perch projecting about 2 inches outside the nest box and 1½ inches inside the box is set approximately ¾ of an inch below the opening. The bottom of the nest consists of a block of wood, 1½ inches thick, with a ¾ inch deep and 4½ inches wide concavity scooped out of it. Whenever possible, the opening of the nest box should face the light. Budgies use no nesting material and the concave shape of the block keeps the eggs collected in the center which makes it easier for the female to brood them. It is convenient to have extra blocks available into which the eggs or the young may be transferred when cleaning the cage.

Budgies are good parents and have no objection to their eggs or young being lifted or handled. However, it is best not to handle them more than necessary. A removable top to the nest box is preferable to hinged sides or back. Too often, in closing the sides, a baby toe or wing is caught and badly injured. Cardboard nest boxes are available commercially. These are inexpensive and may be disposed of when dirty or when breeding is over, thus saving both storage space and a cleaning chore.

The cage itself should be made of ½ inch mesh. There is a commercial mesh of this size which is hexagonal in shape and does not obstruct the view. A wire smaller than this impedes visibility too much, and one larger permits the possibly entry of mice. The same type of wire can be used for the floor of the cage. A pen or tray underneath will catch droppings and help in keeping the cage clean with a minimum of effort.

Budgies will breed better if several cages are kept near each other where the friendly little birds can see their neighbors. Three pairs in separate cages is considered best for good results. However, this does not mean that one or two pairs will not breed well and happily.

Aviaries and Flights. According to Webster's dictionary, an aviary is a house, enclosure, large cage or other place for keeping birds confined, a bird house. In parrakeet breeding, aviary or colony breeding consists basically of releasing a greater or lesser number of pairs of keets in a confined area, providing suitable nest boxes, and letting nature take its course. The disadvantages of this method are obvious. The greatest and most serious fault from the standpoint of improving the breed is that no pedigree records can be kept. Male budgies are notorious adulterers in a situation like this and do not appear to see any harm in carrying on with a light of love while the spouse incubates the eggs.

Nest boxes should be set on hooks in the wall, facing the source of light whenever possible. The hooks should be firm enough so that there is no danger of the box shifting or falling. They should be so arranged that they can be removed easily for cleaning and examination. We have seen aviary walls covered with nest boxes placed so close together that the wall could not be seen, but each budgie knew its own box and flew unerringly to it. They did not need street names or house numbers. To me, all the boxes looked alike, but each clever little bird could tell the difference. Extra nest boxes are essential in an aviary if friction and even bloody fights are to be avoided at mating time. Two nest boxes for each pair is ideal, but if space prohibits this, there should be at least three boxes for every two pairs.

Always avoid having old unattached hens in the aviaries. They are sure to try to take over an occupied nest, pick on the babies and, in general, make life miserable for the other birds. An adult unmated male is not likely to cause trouble, but it is best to avoid the presence of these unattached single birds if possible.

The advantage of colony breeding is that it gives the greatest amount of production within the smallest area. Also, it requires far less work than does the care of the same number of keets paired in individual cages. A number of people who breed parrakeets for the pet market use the colony system. This method is particularly suited to breeding operations in southern California, Texas and Florida. In these warm climates, large wire pens are used to breed parrakeets out of doors all year round. There is little attempt to control operations. Unfit and aged birds are discarded from the breeding pens as they are spotted and the rest are permitted to breed freely.

A variation, which makes use of both methods, is to have a large aviary with a number of small connecting cages around it. These cages, which are provided with nest boxes, are used to mate the birds. Once the eggs are laid, the connecting doors are opened and the birds are allowed to use the flight cage.

It is possible to keep parrakeets outdoors all year round, even if the temperature of the climate in which they are kept drops to 20° F. during the winter. A southern exposure of the aviary, a tight, weatherproof building and adequate ventilation must be provided. The best way to assure adequate ventilation is by having a low air intake at one end of the building and an air outlet situated high on the opposite wall. Care must be taken to prevent the building being drafty. Concrete or metal floors are best, although a sand floor is satisfactory, as it can be raked over several times before it needs to be changed. If the aviary is not too large, it is best to use wire bottom floors. The same hexagonal ½ inch wire that is used for cages may be used for aviaries. This has the distinct advantage of being mouse-proof and permitting easy visibility. While mice do not generally bother the adult birds, they will eat the seed and carry diseases. Rats, on the other hand, will attack birds, so it is wise to make sure that the birdhouse is tight and well constructed with firm foundations.

We are reminded of a man who locked his cat in the aviary one night to rid the place of the rats. In the morning, he still had the rats, but he did not have to worry about his birds—the cat had eaten all of them.

Doors hinged to swing inwards, with a horizontal board set above the inside of the door to prevent birds from flying out when the door is opened, are best. Whenever it is possible, avoid having the doors swing directly into the open. It is much better to have the door open into an alley way or vestibule, so that, should a bird escape, it will not be able to fly far and avoid recapture.

A bird building should have attached outdoor flights in which the birds can exercise on warm days. A shallow pan of water may be provided for those who like bathing, and a bunch of wet carrot tops or wet green lettuce leaves for budgies that like to roll in them. As We have said before, there is a popular fallacy that keets do not like to bathe. While they may hesitate over entering the water at first, once they do try it, they love it. If a few birds in the aviary learn to bathe, the rest will soon follow suit. The water must be shallow and care exercised to avoid the danger of the baby keets drowning themselves. In fact, it is best to avoid both bathing them and letting them bathe themselves until they reach the age of three months.

Diet for Aviary Birds. The diet for aviary birds is much the same as that for cage birds. A 50-50 mixture of Spanish canary seed and the best white millet should be given to the birds at all times. During the winter and breeding season, five percent hulled or steel-cut oats and a five percent quantity of unhulled or brown paddy rice should be added to the above mixture. Cod-liver oil should be added to the seed once a week (eight drops to the pound) and mixed in thoroughly. Greens should be given daily, preferably in the morning, as this gives the bird a chance to fill its crop before settling down for the night. The diet outlined is adequate in most respects, though there is not enough protein for the birds, particularly when there are young birds in the nest. Our suggestion is to supplement this diet with a good grade of dog meal. A small amount of this meal, moistened with skim milk until crumbly, is most beneficial when there are young to be fed. We do not advocate dog biscuits, whole or ground, nor canned dog food. All dog meals are required by law to print the contents of the food on the package, so you should be able to select one that contains no less than 25 percent protein.

Some breeders have trained their keets to eat meal worms (brown caterpillar-shaped larvae of the meal beetle) as a protein supplement. They may be purchased from large pet shops and they will breed readily when kept in a container of bran. The container should be metal and have a perforated metal cover. Budgies do not take readily to eating meal worms and, as the larvae have a hard, chitinous shell, they tend to

Because of the many mutations in color and pattern, the budgie is one of the most variegated and beautiful of birds. Breeders, quick to recognize new phases, have increased the budgie's optical fascination by selecting for and breeding them in a rainbow of brilliant colors.

pack the intestines of the birds and cause severe internal troubles if consumed in large quantities. When a bird is fed individually, the amount it consumes can be controlled, but when a group of birds is fed together, it is impossible to keep some of them from getting more than is good for them. We personally prefer the dog meal to the worms, and feed our birds all they will eat of the former.

Mention should be made of soaking seed for use as a food supplement, especially when the birds have young in the nests. The seeds you want to sprout should not be covered with water, as complete submersion prevents respiration. The seed to be sprouted should be spread on a damp piece of cloth, such as burlap, or a piece of blotting paper. An excellent method of getting seeds to sprout is to place a piece of burlap on an inverted soupdish. Put this in a dish which is kept partially filled with water. The edge of the burlap, dipping into the water, wicks just the right amount of moisture to the seeds. If the seeds fail to sprout when kept in this manner, it is usually because the seeds come from a poor lot. In this case, the source of the seeds should be examined for signs of their being overaged or spoiled.

Aviary Perches. Let us emphasize that all aviary perches should be set firmly in place, care being exercised to see that they are not set one below another, in such a way as to have the birds below soiled by the droppings from the birds above. Avoid swinging perches. Many aviaries use natural wood branches covered with bark in the flights. There is no harm in this provided the wood used is not poisonous. Attempts to have bushes growing in outdoor flights usually end in failure—the birds strip every bit of green as soon as it appears and chew all the succulent young twigs.

This cock, displaying a beautiful straight back and an excellent exhibitor's stance, comes from a stud of which all offspring stand erect and motionless. To create a perfect bird, this cock should be mated to a hen with a huge head and a bull neck. The owner of this bird does not allow any of his stock to fatten, thereby avoiding the development of a roll across the shoulders of his birds, an undesirable feature. This strain has been bred, unbroken by any outside blood, for 28 years, and all possess the same outstanding characteristics.

A pair of budgies should not be allowed to rear more than two clutches of youngsters per season. It is advisable to change the youngsters from one pair of parents to another to produce uniformity in size and numbers. Budgerigars are very cooperative in this respect and do not object when other parents' babies are offered to them.

Serious Breeding

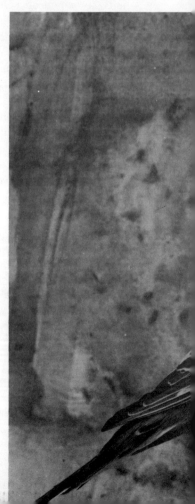

For the person who intends to breed budgies seriously, the best advice we can offer is that the individual have patience. Sit down and think the problem over carefully. Decide what type of breeding will best serve the purpose you have in mind. Do you intend to experiment with color breeding? Are you more interested in experimenting in order to discover more about the genetic background of the budgerigar? Perhaps you have visited a few shows and have decided that you would like to be an exhibitor.

To be a successful breeder of parrakeets, you must be informed. You can obtain and read the standard for the ideal budgerigar, and you can look at pictures and read all kinds of texts, but that is not enough. You must see budgies in the flesh, or rather in the feather. Study the current standard you obtain carefully and then, if possible, visit bird shows. Compare the winners minutely with the standard. If there is anything

you do not understand, do not hesitate to ask the judge or one of the old-timers about it. Most of them are in it for their love of the hobby rather than for any possible monetary returns, and enjoy "strutting their stuff" for the novice. Next to winning first prize at the show, they enjoy making converts. The show standard is a theoretical norm, or standard of perfection which it is hoped all budgies will achieve. Just as we have judges to interpret the law, so shows must have judges to decide which bird most closely approximates perfection. By watching and questioning them, you can learn what points to look for as desirable and what faults are most severely criticized.

By all means join a society. There are a number of local organizations throughout the country.

The national organization is:

The American Budgerigar Society

2 Farnum Road

Warwick, Rhode Island 02888

Selection of Breeding Stock. This stage of the development of your general knowledge of budgies is very important, for on the basis of what you learn you will be buying your breeding stock. Anyone with very little knowledge and a small amount to invest can go out and buy a few pairs of birds and breed them. But if you intend the young from your breeding to be better than the parents you purchased, you must know what you are buying and the breeding goal you have set for yourself.

Rarely, except at great cost, can a show winner be purchased. For the difference in price, it is preferable to purchase several birds closely related to the show winner. Perhaps several of its nest mates are available, or older or younger products of the same mating which produced the winner. It does not matter if they do not look as good as the show winner—with the germ plasm they are carrying, the chances are that with judicious mating and care in selecting their youngsters for future matings, you will produce winners of your own. The exception is the show bird which may be a freak of chance—the one good bird in an otherwise mediocre strain. To determine this you must study the pedigree and see whether that line has produced other winners. It is possible to start with poor birds and build up a winning male or female, but the odds are all against it. It is far better to start with good stock and improve it by careful selection and rigid elimination of the weak and unfit.

Do not try to breed several colors at one time unless you have adequate facilities. It is far better to stick to one color and concentrate on producing birds superior in body, shading and carriage than to have many different colors, all of which are inferior. Even in aviary breeding, it is best to have only birds of one color in a flight. Thus some control, if only a minimum, is exercised.

Should you be fortunate in acquiring adult birds at the proper time of the year, you can start them breeding at once. That their quarters should be ready when they arrive goes without saying. Should only young birds be available, or the purchase be made at a time of year unsuitable for breeding, be patient. Cock budgerigars should not be bred until they are ten months of age, and hens should be a year old. Premature breeding weakens the bird and shortens its life span considerably. It also contributes to weakening the youngsters, as does breeding out of season. By breeding at the wrong time of year, the birds' systems are thrown out of kilter. The babies are born at the wrong time for maximum development, and, when the proper season does arrive, the parent birds will be exhausted. Whenever possible, separate the sexes so that they will be in top condition when breeding time comes.

Mating. All matings should first be made on paper, that is, written out. Compare the good points and bad of each bird and select the pairs which will give the best chance for successful youngsters.

Usually, mating is simple. Even a budgie which has had the same mate for a number of years rarely makes any objection when a new mate is provided and the old one kept out of sight. The female should be kept in the mating cage for several days before introducing the male. Do not provide a nest box until you have seen the birds mating or are reasonably sure by their actions that mating has taken place. This practice will help prevent the hen's laying infertile eggs in her hurry to get started.

Occasionally a pair of budgies kept alone will hesitate about mating. The presence of one or more pairs placed in adjoining, visible cages helps overcome this. A second method worth trying is to place each alone, in adjoining cages. Wait until they try to get to each other through the bars, and then put them together. Should you have a pair which persist in their refusal, then it is best to try different mates.

Always be sure that your birds are in top condition when you try to mate them—eyes bright, feathers hard, bright and shiny—in short, active and lively birds that swagger around as though they owned the world. Never try to mate a pair of parrakeets until all signs of the molt are past.

It is just as inexpensive and considerably easier to breed from top quality birds as from inferior budgerigars. The difference comes in the pride which you can take in raising a nest of good young ones, which is only possible when the parents are good. There is always a market for good birds, while the inferior ones go begging.

Nesting. Assuming that all factors are favorable, mating should take place within a few days after the pair is placed together. It is not necessary to use any nesting material, although some breeders feel that a handful of pine sawdust helps keep the nest clean.

The first egg is usually laid about eight days after the actual mating takes place. After that, an egg is laid on alternate days until the clutch is completed. This can be as many as nine or even more eggs, although such a large clutch is not usual. The male feeds the female while she sits on the nest. The young hatch out seventeen days after the egg is laid. This means, of course, that the chicks hatch out every other day. When there is a large number of eggs, it is possible for the first chick hatched to be two weeks old before the last eggs have hatched. In actual practice this seems to do no harm, all chicks being fed and reared together.

Many breeders make it a practice to remove the first three eggs as they are laid and replace them with glass eggs. The eggs which were removed are kept on end on a bed of sawdust or absorbent cotton at room temperature and turned twice daily to prevent the embryo from settling. Taking away more eggs than this seems to prevent the earliest ones from hatching. When the eggs removed are from the second round, and chicks are in the nest, glass eggs are unnecessary. Replace the eggs on the same day the hen has laid them. Warm the eggs in your hand for a few minutes before replacing them.

When quite a number of breeding pairs are kept, it is possible to re-assort the youngsters themselves once they hatch. Budgerigars are very tolerant of changes, accepting a strange baby with the greatest equanimity. The older babies can be taken from one nest and the youngest from another and switched, so that the parents are feeding babies all of about the same size. Changing over is also practiced when one nest is very large and another exceptionally small. For instance, should one nest have eight babies or eggs and another only three, it is quite practical to take two from the larger and give them to the smaller. The parents do not seem to mind in the least.

To help maintain records, eggs may be marked with colored nail polish. This can be used to mark the date they were laid, which enables one to foretell the hatching date. It is also convenient when swapping eggs with other nests, so that you can tell the paternity of the eggs and also ensure that they are placed with eggs of approximately the same age. Colorless nail polish can be used successfully to repair minor cracks in eggs if the inner membrane is not torn.

Banding. Each baby should be banded with a seamless metal band when it is four or five days old. This ring bears the year of birth, a serial number, and the initials of the society issuing it. The band forms the bird's own permanent registration. It can be placed on the bird only during the first few days of its life while the foot is small and soft—the fourth or fifth day after hatching. Once the foot has grown, it is impossible to slip off the old band, or slip on a new one. A very careful record must be kept of all chicks as they are banded. This is essential to the keeping of the pedigrees, without which no successful strain can be established and maintained.

To band the youngsters, pass the three long toes through the band. Slide it up over the ball of the foot as far as it will go and pull the last toe through with a small pointed stick. If you have delayed too long, or if the foot is unusually large, a little vaseline will aid in getting the band on.

Care and Cleaning of the Baby Budgies. Regular inspections of the nest box are important and necessary. Remove any eggs which fail to hatch, since the growing chicks will break them and make a mess. Having extra wooden bottom blocks is a great convenience. It takes only a few minutes to remove the babies, slip in a clean block and replace the young. Should the feet or bills of the babies become plastered with dry dirt, do not try to pull it off. Soak the feet in warm water until the dirt is loosened. Wash the face gently when necessary. Tender toe nails can be pulled off and a soft beak can be malformed unless care is exercised. Pay particular attention to the rump of the bird. The anal opening of the baby can very readily become clogged with soft droppings. These should be carefully washed away. If there are dirty feathers, these can be clipped with a scissors. Some birds are messy feeders and plaster the faces of their young and even the sides of the boxes with food. Be particularly watchful with these and clean them more often. All moving and cleaning of nest boxes should be done early in the day as this gives both babies and parents a chance to settle down before the night.

Difficulties That Might Be Met. As we have already said, budgerigars are, as a rule, very good parents. Occasionally you will find a hen which neglects her youngsters. In that case it is best to distribute them among several nests. Should no other nests be available, it is often possible to remove the hen, and leave the male to take over alone. It is very common for one parent to take over by itself when something has happened to the other.

There are records of male budgies which work too hard at feeding a large family. They soon show signs that their own health has suffered. Should this happen, it is best to separate the male from the family for a few days and feed him well. As soon as he recovers, he can be returned to the nest.

An egg-bound hen, that is, a hen unable to lay the egg which has

Proud parents take care of their youngsters even after they have left the nest.

The young birds shown here are about 11 days old. As the budgies are hatched on different days, they do not all leave the nest simultaneously either.

formed inside her, will be found lying on the floor of the cage or nest box. She will be all puffed up and when the feathers are blown away from the abdomen, it will appear to be swollen. Treatment for this difficulty will be found in the section on "Common Budgie Diseases."

Records. We cannot stress often enough the vital importance of keeping records, particularly when youngsters are being switched from nest to nest. Sometimes it is possible to place babies in a nest with parents which could not possibly have bred them, as for instance, placing a blue youngster in a nest of whites. Opalines can be distinguished in the nest at a very tender age by a green or blue luminous cast on the forehead.

When thirty days old, the young begin to leave the nest. It is best to keep them with the parents for another eight to ten days. At the end of that time, it is advisable to separate them and place the babies in a separate cage or aviary with other youngsters.

Another good way to end the breeding season for a pair is to remove the hen when the second set of youngsters is about two weeks old. The male, as suggested before, will raise the youngsters alone and then, when they are old enough to eat alone, the father can be retired for a well-earned rest.

As the size of the feet of the individual chicks varies, it is necessary to watch the youngsters from the age of about five days old onward so that their feet do not become too big for the bands to pass over.

Birds that look as lovely as these pictured at left and below present no problem in being sold.

Disposal of Surplus Budgies

At the end of the breeding season it is well to pause and take stock. Look over the new crop of babies. Judge them in their own right and also judge the parents. How successful were they in raising their young? How good are the youngsters they have raised? If a particular mating failed to produce any good young, or, as a breeder may say, "failed to nick," plan to try different mates the following year.

Dispose ruthlessly of all superfluous or inferior stock. Keep only the best for breeding next year and the finest birds for showing. Plan ahead to see whether you had best bring some new blood into the aviary. If so, start looking around early. Visit the shows and other breeders until you find the type you want at a price you can afford. All too often waiting too long means that you must accept an inferior bird at a superior price. No breeder is eager to sell a bird at the start of the breeding season—not after he has held it all year just so that he can breed from it himself.

Defective Stock. All birds which are defective physically or are in poor health should be destroyed. This is a blanket statement. It is no kindness to a poor, weak, deformed budgerigar to allow it to drag out its life in suffering and misery. Very rarely is a good home found for these misfits. They are tossed from place to place as not worth the price of feeding. Eventually they perish miserably.

It is a grave mistake in judgment and ethics to dispose of such birds to the pet market. There is always some novice, ignorant of what constitutes a good budgie, who will pay a few dollars for a bargain bird. He usually finds out in the end that he has been duped, and that certainly does nothing to enhance the reputation of the breeder who made the sale.

Selling Birds. There are always a certain number of youngsters at the end of each season which are strong, healthy birds, but which suffer from some slight defect that makes them unsuitable for showing. These find a ready market as pets. The pet market is the greatest outlet the dealer has today for surplus birds. At present writing, it appears that it will be years before the market is glutted. As more and more people become acquainted with the charms of the little budgerigar, its popularity grows and the demand increases.

Advertisements in cage bird periodicals, pet magazines and local papers will serve to dispose of all the birds you can produce.

Most large breeders prefer to sell directly to pet shops rather than to individuals. All of the business can be transacted by mail and the birds shipped in quantity. Although the price charged a pet shop is of necessity less than that charged an individual, this loss is more than compensated for by the convenience of bulk sales.

Babies intended for sale in the pet market can be removed from their parents at about five weeks of age. They should be kept with other youngsters in cages for about a week to accustom them to being on their own. It is better to cover the bottom of the cage with seed rather than to depend on food hoppers.

Shipping Birds. At six weeks of age they are ready to be shipped. Shipment is made in cardboard boxes, the size depending on the number of birds to be sent. A cardboard carton 24" long by 12" wide by 8" high serves nicely for a dozen birds. Any cardboard carton in good condition can be used for shipping keets. Cut a five-inch square in one side of the carton. Over this opening staple, or fasten securely with wide gummed tape, a piece of ¼" wire or plastic mesh. Cover the floor with a mixture of equal parts of white millet, canary seed and hulled oats. Place several orange quarters in the box for liquid, and seal the box all around. It is unnecessary and inadvisable to provide water, since it would probably spill and soak a hole in the box. The orange serves adequately to quench the birds' thirst.

To put the birds in the box, cut a flap in the side about four inches long and three inches wide. This flap can be lifted to place the birds in one at a time. When they are all safely inside, a little gummed tape will seal the flap very nicely. This method is much more convenient than opening the box top and having a bird pop out every time you try to put one in.

Whenever possible, ship by air. The time saved is certainly worth the small additional charge. There are certain small details which will help to save a little on the freight bill. As most air freight is billed by cubic measurements as well as weight, use the smallest box consistent with the birds' safety. When you find it necessary to ship several boxes, tie them together and have them charged as one. This will eliminate a separate minimum charge for each box.

All boxes should have at least two labels securely fastened to each of them, giving the name and address of the shipper, as well as the full name and address of the consignee. It is a good idea to write on these tags: ON ARRIVAL, CALL ———, giving the telephone number of the consignee. This often makes it possible for the birds to be picked up hours before a truck would normally deliver them. In bad weather this could mean the difference between life and death. The shipping carton should also be prominently marked: THIS SIDE UP—HANDLE WITH CARE—LIVE BIRDS—KEEP OUT OF HOT SUN—KEEP FROM EXTREME COLD. We strongly advise notifying the consignee in advance, of the date you expect to ship and the means of transportation you intend to employ, so that cages may be prepared and the local freight agent asked to look for the shipment.

When preparing a shipment, always consider the person to whom you are sending the birds. When he receives them, will they be the sort of specimens you, yourself, would want to find in shipments coming to you?

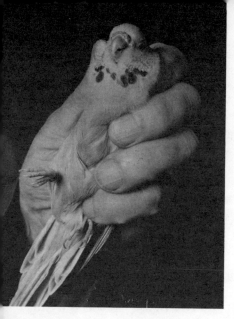

The bird at left being held here for inspection is a good healthy specimen. Healthy birds must have a well-balanced diet in order to maintain good health. Below: Nutrition is an important factor in the development of the budgie chick, especially when the bird is beginning to feather.

Budgie Nutrition

The problem of nutrition is a very complicated one. It was not until about the year 1900 that scientists began to concern themselves with nutrition and the effect of the diet upon the body. There is still much to be discovered in this field, but a great deal has already been done, and there are certain basic facts that are of vital importance to us as budgerigar owners.

While many successful breeders pay no attention to the scientific aspect of the diet which they feed their birds, nevertheless they succeed in rearing healthy youngsters. This is because over the years they have learned by trial and error which diet gives the best results, even though they do not know why this is so. It is mainly for the person who wants to know "why" that this chapter is written.

Mechanics of Digestion. However, before we go into the "why" of budgie nutrition, it is best, for more complete understanding, to study the "how."

The budgie has a powerful hooked beak with which it cracks the seed it eats. A budgie, unlike domestic fowl, does not eat the entire seed, but discards the husk and eats only the kernel. The seed is passed from the tongue down the throat by stretching the neck and jerking the head. The food goes down the gullet, being soaked with saliva on the way, until it reaches an enlargement known as the crop. This is actually a pre-digestion area where the food is soaked and softened in preparation.

It is in the crop that both the male and female budgie parents produce the milk which they feed to their youngsters. This milk develops toward the end of the incubation period and, in feeding their chicks, is regurgitated from the crop. It is not actually "milk" as we know it, but a lumpy mixture of protein and fat. The feeding process consists of the young placing its bill inside that of the parent bird. The food is then forced directly down the gullet of the youngster. It is not uncommon to have two youngsters feed each other partially digested food when they are taken away from the parents at an early age.

Below the crop the gullet continues to the gizzard. This lower section of the gullet corresponds to the mammalian stomach. It is in this passage that the digestive juices are secreted and mixed with food. From there the food passes into the gizzard.

As most people know, a bird has no teeth. Its food is swallowed whole, along with bits of gravel, lime, grit and the like. The gizzard is the organ which churns and grinds all this together until it is a soaked and doughy mass which can be utilized by the body.

Between the intestines proper and the gizzard is a thickened tube properly known as the duodenum. Into the duodenum two tubes discharge their contents.

Bile, which is manufactured by the liver and stored in the gall bladder, acts upon fats to split them into globules so tiny that they are invisible; it also has a laxative action. The other gland conducts more starch-digesting substances from the pancreas. This converts starches into dextrin which is then converted into glucose by another substance excreted by the small intestine. In this way, the carbohydrates are transformed into absorbable nourishment. Proteins and fats are also reduced to their component parts—amino acids and fatty acids—into forms that permit them to pass through the intestinal wall into the lymph and blood.

In the intestines, the absorption takes place along the entire wall. The area of this organ is greatly increased by tiny projections called *villi* which line the walls. These projections, while minute themselves, are sufficiently numerous to increase the absorption area tremendously. Food is moved through the intestine by a wave-like series of expansions and contractions known as peristaltic movement. What is left of the food after it has travelled through the small intestine is deposited through a valve into the large intestine, where it may contain large amounts of water. Here water is absorbed and here a huge growth of bacteria takes place. In budgies, as in all birds, the urine and feces are excreted together from the same opening. In healthy budgies the feces are semisolid, the center being dark green and the rim white.

Now that we have seen how food is digested, let us see what is necessary to maintain a budgerigar in a state of good health. *Water* is essential to life. As much as 70 per cent of the body is water. Water is used as water and does not combine chemically with other substances. As water it comes into the body, as water it is used for carrying out waste products, for bathing the cells, for carrying useful substances, and so forth, and as water it passes out of the body. In addition to its internal value, water, by its evaporation, helps to regulate body temperature.

Although many pets do not seem to drink water, actually getting enough for their purposes from the foods which they eat, nevertheless it is advisable to have it available to them at all times. For birds newly arrived and whose droppings appear to be loose, it is best to boil the water.

Essentials in the Bird's Diet. *Minerals* compose about 6 percent of the bird's body. The following are the principal ones. *Calcium*—90 percent of body calcium is in the bone and feathers. It is also the principal ingredient of egg shells. You can supply calcium to your birds by occasional bread and milk feedings, oyster shell grit, crushed egg shell, and by having cuttle fish bone always at hand. Lack of sufficient calcium results, among other things, in soft shelled eggs.

Proteins are a second group of essentials. Amino acids are the component parts of proteins. Proteins differ among themselves in that they contain different combinations of amino acids.

There are twenty-two of these amino acids, but only ten of these, so far as we know, are essential to the diet. Amino acids have been called the building blocks of the body. Their primary function is building body tissues, and in the case of birds, feathers are composed almost entirely of protein.

Not all protein is in a form which can be utilized by the body. It is not enough to know that a food contains protein; we must also know whether this protein is in a form which can be utilized by the bird's body.

As the seeds which we feed our budgies are notoriously deficient in suitable proteins, it is essential that we supplement the diet with such foods as milk, either powdered or liquid, egg yolk, and alfalfa leaf meal. A good grade of dog meal, moistened and fed fresh daily, is a very valuable source of protein as well as of other dietary essentials.

Carbohydrates are derived from plants. As all seeds are rich in carbohydrates, we need have no concern about their availability in our bird's diet. This is also true of *fat*. Canary seed, for instance, when analyzed is found to be 14 percent protein, 55 percent carbohydrate, and 6 percent fat. White millet seed is 11 percent protein, 60 percent carbohydrate, and 4 percent fat. Rape seed, which many breeders add to the diet of breeding birds and young keets, is 19 percent fat. Because of its high fat content it should be fed sparingly.

Seeds which have been kept moist on a layer of cloth, burlap or blotting paper until sprouted, are valuable as a dietary supplement for all keets. This is particularly good for breeding birds, youngsters, and sick birds.

When seed is kept moist, water enters the seed rapidly and causes a noticeable swelling. All of the soluble substances in the seed are dissolved. The enzymes go to work speeding along the process of respiration and digestion. The stored foods begin to digest. Starch changes to sugar, and fats to fatty acids. Proteins are broken down into their component parts, the amino acids. In these forms they can be absorbed directly in the nutrition of the animal or bird which eats them.

All diets are predicated on clean, fresh foods. Naturally, spoiled or moldy seeds and wilted greens, far from being beneficial, are a definite menace to the health. They do not supply the essentials for which they were fed, and may even be sufficiently spoiled to be toxic. Under ordinary circumstances a bird will not eat spoiled food, but, confined in an area with no other choice, it is forced to try to get along on what is placed before it. The danger is particularly acute in the case of egg and milk foods. These should be mixed fresh just prior to feeding them. In hot weather, do not let them stand for more than two hours, and wash the receptacles well after they are emptied.

Many adult birds manage to struggle along on a maintenance diet. However, this is a poor policy to follow. These birds are invariably the first to die when illness strikes, since they have no reserves of strength on which to fall back. As pets they are certainly inferior for they often do not have enough energy to be playful.

As for the baby budgie, it is definitely a cruelty to withhold dietary supplements. We have had any number of budgies brought to us by despairing pet lovers. The story has too often been the same. They have been sold or given a bird and a box of seed and sent out like babes in the woods on their own. In almost every case, when the essential items mentioned in this chapter were added to their pet's diet, the change was almost miraculous. Within a short time, often as little as a week, a baby which was thin, listless, feeble, and lacked all interest in life, picked up. Feathers took on a new sheen, body carriage improved, the bird began to chatter, the eyes cleared, the dull look disappeared and a new life began both for the bird and for its owner.

Fats that are found in natural foods are utilized by budgies just as they are used by all animate creatures. Fortunately we need not make provisions for fats in the diets of parrakeets because grains contain all the essential fatty acids in abundance. Fatty acids are the components of fats, as amino acids are the components of proteins.

Vitamins are organic dietary substances small quantities of which are essential to the normal functioning of the body.

Vitamin A is necessary to birds. Without it they develop severe symptoms including inflammation of the conjunctiva of the eye and sterility. Plenty of dark green leaves, whole milk, grated carrot, and egg yolk, as well as cod-liver oil (8 drops per pound of seed, renewed weekly) will supply all that the birds require.

B complex is found so abundantly in grain that one seldom sees evidences of deficiency.

That is, one seldom sees it when the grain fed is fresh. All too many times we are shown budgies suffering from B deficiency because the seed they were getting was too old and dry. The seed for budgies should be principally white millet, which is a rounded light yellow or creamy white seed, and canary seed, which should be shiny and plump. Do not feed your budgie a mixture which contains large quantities of small *red* millet.

When in doubt as to the visibility of the seed you are feeding, plant some in a flower pot and see how much of it sprouts. Some seeds we have tested have shown as little as 10% germination. How good can these be for the bird they are fed to? A safe procedure is to get some brewer's yeast at the drug store. A pinch of this in the seed cup every other day will insure an adequate supply of the B complex vitamins.

Vitamin C is manufactured within the body of the bird.

Vitamin D is manufactured by birds when they have enough sunlight. Birds kept indoors, behind glass panes which filter out the actinic rays of the sun, require some supplemental form of this vitamin. Cod-liver oil is an excellent source of this vitamin, as well as of A.

Vitamin E is found in all whole grains. Birds must have it or they develop a mental derangement. The female also needs it to develop fertile eggs, but probably the male has no need of vitamin E for fertility.

Vitamin K is another vitamin essential to the diet. Lack of this vitamin results in inability of the blood to clot. Green foods are an excellent source of vitamin K.

Phosphorus is found in the bones, blood and muscles. It is used for bone building, carbohydrate and fat metabolism, as a component part of blood and the liquid content of tissues, and as a rickets preventative. The incidence of rickets is high, particularly among birds raised in the winter and whose parents were not supplied with a proper diet. Phosphorus is available in milk and is abundant in whole grains. A normal diet supplies as much as is necessary of this essential mineral.

Iron composes only a tiny fraction of the body weight. It is essential as a component of red blood cells and to transport oxygen in the blood. An insufficiency produces anemia. Egg yolk and green vegetables are the principal sources of iron for cage birds.

Potassium is a body-fluid regulator, helps regulate blood, and is necessary for muscular function. Green vegetables will supply this.

Sodium and *chlorine* are both essential to the birds, as is *iodine*. All three can be supplied by dropping a few crystals of iodized salt into the drinking water every other day.

Sulphur, essential to body regulation, is found in egg yolk and in grains. It is unnecessary to add any additional sulphur to a normal diet, which contains an ample supply.

Manganese, although found in grains, is sometimes lacking in sufficient quantity in the diet. Symptoms of manganese deficiency are failure of eggs to hatch, overgrown beaks, malformed bones and slipped tendons. If this lack is not corrected in a young bird, there is no cure for it as an adult. The addition of a minute amount of manganese sulfate to the grit is sufficient.

In addition to these, small amounts of other so-called "trace minerals" are required. A grain diet supplemented daily with fresh, well-washed greens will supply all these.

Vitamin A deficiency often causes a watery fluid to run out of the nostrils and cake around the beak. These symptoms are the same as those for bird pox, so a proper diagnosis should be speedily made before treatment.

If you are a real bird lover, you will do everything in your power to protect these birds from any hazards.

*How Not
to Lose a
Pet Budgie*

As a parrakeet owner, there are always certain precautions which you must observe to keep from losing your pet. Many a beloved parrakeet has been lost when forethought would have saved it. Here are several easy ways to lose one:

To Cats. While it is true that birds generally stay away from the family cat, there are times when a particularly avid killer will surmount difficulties and tip over the cage, reach through the bars and kill the bird. If you live where a cat could jump to your window sill, keep all unscreened windows closed to the room in which your pet is caged. If you put it out for airing, take care the cage is placed where no cat could reach it. And do not trust the family cat who has never showed any interest in your bird, and leave it in the room with the budgie.

This normal dark green cock is excellent in type and stance. The head is very good, also. The only drawbacks of this elegant specimen are the slightly patchy coloring and the fact that the mask and spots are a little uneven.

This small yellow face skyblue lacks a frontal rise and has spots that are too small. Even these faults, though, cannot take away from the very good even color and markings that make this bird so attractive.

Fine color, good type, correct markings and good stance all make this normal violet so distinguished. Unfortunately, this lovely bird lacks in top skull, depth of mask and in the size of the spots, making him less than perfect.

Good type through-out can be attributed to this charming, normal light green budgie. This bird has a good head, but slightly patchy color. The mask could be deeper, and you can notice that the spots are irregular.

It is not killing alone which you need fear; many a budgie has been so tumbled about in its cage or so terrified that it was never the same afterward.

Through Open Windows. It is easy to come to trust your pet too much. Some budgies will return like homing pigeons, it is true, but most of them become so bewildered on finding themselves in the great outdoors, they simply fly and fly aimlessly. We have told you how to capture one which has escaped—if you catch it at all. We have known them to be caught by predatory birds before the owners could recover their pets.

From Spraying. Never leave a budgie in a room you are spraying for mosquitoes or flies. Many valuable birds are killed annually this way. Some sprays are harmless and even beneficial when put on feathers, but some kinds, when inhaled, produce death rapidly. Put your bird out of the room and do not bring it back until you have aired the room after the insects are dead.

Temperature Changes. Budgies can stand a fairly high degree of heat but they die if overheated and, if used to a warm room, may die when chilled. One of the most common causes of overheating is leaving the bird's cage in the bright summer sun, with no shade. The owner puts the cage there when there is perhaps no sun, and forgets the window will later on be in the sun's full glare.

Hot damp rooms, like kitchens, may cause loss of feathers if not a true molt.

Budgies accustomed to gradual temperature changes are very hardy. Drafts cause pneumonia which is often fatal.

Electric Wires. Because of their inquisitive natures and love of working on an object with their strong beaks, budgies sometimes bite through electric wires and the flash from the short circuit may badly burn their beaks and frighten them into a shock, if it does not kill them. If you give your bird the freedom of a room where you are not present to keep an eye on it, leave no hot electric wires where the bird can chew them.

From Poisoning. Fresh paint has poisoned many a pet bird. It is generally the pigment in the paint rather than the lead, but be sure anyway not to leave freshly painted objects about. Once the paint is thoroughly dry, it is usually safe.

Not taking proper care of your budgie can be the worst hazard he faces. The overgrowth of the lower beak on this bird could be the result of a vitamin D deficiency and the lack of cuttlefish bone.

A normal mauve budgie. This grayish shade is not as popular as the brilliant blues, for example, but it is of great value to the color breeder, and can command a good price from large commercial breeders.

This beautiful normal gray is a near-perfect example of its variety. Gray is not a sex-linked, so both hens and cocks can be gray if at least one parent is gray. The normal gray pictured here is qualified as an exhibition bird.

A normal graywing skyblue. An outstanding feature of the graywing, which adds to its beautiful appearance, is the broad wing markings. Graywings are not to be as heavily marked as the normal gray.

This slightly heavy whitewing skyblue has a faulty stance because of its weight. Its coloring is excellent.

Beak deformities like the one shown above should always be checked by a veterinarian immediately, and should be treated with great care. The birds pictured at right are suffering from French Molt, a feather disease which is being linked to poor nutrition. These birds are a sorry sight compared to healthy birds who have benefited from a proper diet.

Common Budgie Diseases

The effects of the majority of budgie diseases are so similar on the appearance of the bird that the best experts cannot tell to look at your pet what disease it has. So it is beyond the scope of this book and of little interest to the budgie owner what specific disease the bird has. It might be any one of a dozen or more, including ornithosis. Only a pathological examination can determine the cause of death, and sometimes even that cannot.

You do not need to be told when your budgie is sick. It shows it plainly. Ruffled feathers, loss of appetite, sometimes excessive thirst, perhaps convulsions, watery discolored droppings, discharge from eyes and nose. Indeed, you need no doctor to tell you.

The graywing cobalt, one of three in the blue series, has long been established. The show bird breeder of this color need only try to perfect this variety.

A perfect yellow face graywing is one of the most desired colors in budgies. This mutation can also be carried by birds in the green series.

This opaline gray green has excellent color and markings. A change in pattern accompanied by a slight reduction in the basic body color is a result of the opaline mutation.

The opaline olive green, one of the many opaline mutations, is becoming increasingly popular in the United States and in other budgie loving countries. This bird has good color but uneven spots.

MEDICATION

Of the generalized diseases, fortunately a good many yield to aureomycin and streptomycin. These antibiotics are most easily given in the drinking water. A sick bird will usually consume part of a teaspoonful of water a day. Theoretically a bird needs only three to five milligrams of aureomycin twice daily, but twice or three times that amount will do no harm. A 100 milligram capsule is the size to buy. Dissolve one-fifth of its contents in a teaspoonful of water and give only that water to the sick budgie. If, after it has consumed the half spoonful during the day, then give it additional water but leave none with the bird overnight. Next day give the medicine again and continue for one day after the bird appears well. It may require five days of dosing.

In almost all of the budgie ailments where generalized disease needs treatment, remember you are managing a tropical bird. Therefore, the temperature must be tropical. Place a drape over three sides of the cage. Put a thermometer in it and if you have no other means of keeping the temperature up, hang an electric light in the cage. Temperatures ranging from 80° to 90°F. seem to increase chances of the bird's recovery.

Some students advise giving no food other than that which a sick bird will eat naturally while some advise concentrated foods. Judging by apparent results, feeding small amounts of sugar is an excellent procedure. Honey is a mixture of sugars and is not repellent. If you give it, thin the honey with enough water to allow it to be fed with a medicine dropper. Pick up a drop of the mixture at a time and administer it slowly. Ten drops a day may make a great difference in the bird's recovery.

Caution. Whenever administering liquids, do not attempt to give a drop at a time with a full medicine dropper because it is too easy to give too much and choke your pet. Take a drop at a time into the dropper and administer that to the bird. Then, take up another drop.

PSITTACOSIS-ORNITHOSIS

There is such a general popular dread of psittacosis (parrot fever) and because that dread has done much to act as a brake on the even greater popularity of budgies, there are some facts about it you should know. First, it is a very rare disease in parrot-family birds raised in captivity. If your budgie becomes sick, the chances are that it has some other disease. As already stated, it is difficult to distinguish it by external appearance from the other more common diseases. Symptoms vary. In some of the epidemics, the loss to breeders has been close to 100 percent, in others, scarcely one in twenty-five birds died. Some fall dead off their perches, some lose weight and condition rapidly and die in convulsions.

Time was when the disease was called *psittacosis.* The student of bird diseases now calls it *ornithosis,* because it infects all species of birds. Some students hold that birds of the parrot family have their own special strain; others doubt it.

Great numbers of wild birds, pigeons and poultry have it, recover and become carriers. Many species of mammals may have it. Human beings are no exception. It is wise, therefore, to keep parrakeets away from contact with any bird and human carriers. Never hang a cage out of doors where sparrows or pigeons could defecate on or into it. The virus may even spread in dust blown about.

Ornithosis in humans is a disease of adults; children are almost never infected. It is curable, being one of the few virus diseases that can be overcome with a drug.

Of the other general diseases, budgies may have paratyphoid, cholera, Newcastle disease, pullorum, tuberculosis, pseudotuberculosis, diphtheria, erysipelas, aspergellosis, pox, malaria and others.

Of the recognizable specific diseases which you may be able to identify, there are the following:

Infectious Coryza. Several diseases produce swelling of the membranes of the head and discharge from nose and eyes. There is one *infectious coryza* which produces symptoms much like those of a cold in human beings. The eyes may seem to protrude if the swelling behind them is great. The budgie sneezes a great deal to clear its nose and upper respiratory tract.

Wheezing. Then there is the parrakeet with a wheeze much like that heard in asthmatic persons. The bird wheezes both on inspiration and expiration. This condition may be a symptom of a disease or simply the result of another disease such as diphtheria which produces the abnormal growth of tissue. When it is not a disease symptom, wheezing often yields when a diet of laxative food and vegetables are fed.

Urinary Ailments. If your budgie drinks an abnormal amount of water, if it discharges such an abnormally large amount of urine that its feces are liquid, if it seems to want more succulent foods than seeds, look out for kidney disease. At the first signs of such symptoms it pays to treat with aureomycin.

DEFICIENCY DISEASES

The loss of parrakeets by improper diet is much less than in the case of many other birds, because the excellent instructions furnished by food purveyors are generally followed.

When a hen budgie lays soft shelled eggs or the young grow with crooked legs or soft beaks (parrot beaks), a deficiency is probably to be blamed. This could be due to calcium or vitamin D. If nestlings grow

This gorgeous white-wing cobalt is an excellent example of its variety. The high quality of care that this bird has received is evident by its appearance. The importance of proper nutrition for a bird cannot be overemphasized.

The normal cinnamon violet pictured here has a beautiful soft contrast of warm and cold coloration. This is a very beautiful variety becoming more and more established, especially in the high-quality standards for exhibition.

This yellow wing dark green budgie does not have the ideal straight back necessary to meet the postion standard in exhibition. His eyes are bright and alert, however, another important standard, and his color is good.

The normal cinnamon graywing pictured here is a lovely bird distinguished by the warm brownish wings markings, characteristic of all true cinnamons. Many birds of this variety are reaching the highest standards of exhibition.

with slipped tendons, the deficiency could be magnesium. If eggs fail to hatch some deficiency is often at the bottom. Grain that is grown in iodine-deficient soils can produce goiter in budgies. Poor coloration, unthriftiness, stunted growth can come from inadequate proteins in the diet.

Budgies with eye inflammation, or if they are sterile, may be wanting in vitamin A. Birds reared out of the sun's active rays can and often do develop rickets.

Yet not one of these deficiencies can develop if you feed good quality whole grains, hard boiled egg yolk, milk, green vegetables and a very little cod-liver oil.

PARASITIC DISEASES

Almost all of the parasitic diseases of the internal sorts which mature budgies contract are those passed to them by wild birds sitting on the cages hung outside to air. One of the worst of these is coccidiosis, easily cured by one of the sulfa drugs your veterinarian will gladly give you.

Roundworms, tapeworms, flukes, blood infections with certain blood parasites, even mouth infections (canker) caused by a single-celled organism are not unknown to parrakeets. Your veterinarian can detect them by microscopic examinations.

The external parasites are among the most troublesome ailments of pet budgies. The birds are usually infested when they are purchased because there is no source of infestation for the several body and feather lice and mites in the average home.

Today it is becoming increasingly easy to eradicate them. Flea powder dusted into the feathers eliminate most of these external feather or skin chewers or blood suckers. There are also several excellent sprays to be had which are unusually effective and, strangely enough, the birds do not mind the fizzing sound of the mist as much as one would expect.

OIL DUCT OBSTRUCTION

This is a real trouble, fairly common and most annoying to budgies. If your pet spends what seems to you too much time with its bill working at the base of its tail, and you know the bird is reasonably free from insects, part the feathers and examine the little nipple through which the oil glands discharge. If you find a brownish or blackish plug in it, massage it and try to work the plug out with the eye end of a needle, and the oil can flow again.

FRENCH MOLT

This condition is the most talked about ailment of parrakeets and deservedly so. Certainly the last word as to its cause has not been spoken. If one reviews the studies made by careful workers, one finds several causes held accountable for the condition.

French molt may be a catch-all term used to designate all sorts of feather troubles.

More specifically it is used to describe a feather condition in which the bird constantly molts. It is continually growing new feathers and losing old ones. The quills are soft, pull out easily and if opened, are found to be filled with a dark substance. The entire bird begins to look ragged and bare patches appear.

So-called crawlers, creepers or runners seem to have their troubles concentrated in the wing primaries and long tail feathers. These never quite seem to completely develop, but fall out when about two thirds grown. The feathers on examination are seen to be ruffled and uneven, quite different from normal primaries and tails. Such birds are rarely capable of flight, but develop strong legs and can run like chickens, hence the name. About fifty percent of the crawlers die by the time they are six months old. The remainder may recover, or may live their lives out as runners. In spite of this handicap, many of them make good pets and excellent talkers. However, a normal full feathered bird is definitely to be preferred. Neither molt is the same as feather pulling.

As to causes, four theories have been advanced: 1. Heredity, 2. Nutritional deficiency, 3. Mites, 4. Bacterial or viral agents.

In analyzing the evidence supporting the conclusions of those who have done the best work, the mite theory is incontestable. A species of harvest mite was definitely implicated in one kind of molt. But, is that the only cause?

It is quite amazing that some molters are found in the same nest with nestlings which never develop the condition. Some students claim to have cured the ailment by changing food, and that it never returned. Was that, then, true French molt?

Heredity as a cause is doubted because when it occurs, it does not occur in proper proportions to be typical. Sometimes a pair of normal parents will have a nest full of molters. Unfortunately, the subject has not been well enough studied. Even runners can be bred and have been known to produce normals.

On the basis of what we know, the fairly liberal use of insecticide harmless to the birds should be used in the nest boxes and on the young birds whenever there is a suspicion of molt existing. If a young bird you have purchased becomes a molter, return it to the seller at once as most

This olive green budgie is representative of the darkest color variety in the green series. The olive green is valuable to breeders, although not as popular to pet fanciers, because it can produce such unique colors as a bronze shade (olive green x cinnamon).

This yellow wing light green has a good straight back, but is slightly heavy. The beak is well tucked in, and the tail feathers, properly colored pale grass green, are straight and tight.

The graywing olive green has long tail feathers darker in proportion to the rest of its body.

Normal yellow. Show standards demand that this variety be as free of any green as possible.

sellers stand back of their birds. If you cannot return it, try frequent insecticidal sprays and see if as the new feathers grow in, they are not normal.

Inquiring of breeders who have or have not had the condition appear among their birds, one is struck with the apparent correlation of diet with French molt. One breeder of long experience and with no French molt has always fed liberally of whole eggs. Another, in whose aviary the condition frequently has appeared, seldom has fed eggs or anything but seeds and greens. Another has used a certain dry dog food and no molt has been seen. These foods contain complete assortments of essential amino acids, especially cystine and methionine—two which contain sulphur, a mineral in which the average budgie diet is often low.

If lack of sulphur is the cause or one of the causes of French molt, then perhaps budgie diets need more animal protein. Sulphur, as such, is not assimilated to any extent in its pure form. In natural combination in the two amino acids, it is well utilized by the body.

FIRST AID TO YOUR PET PARRAKEET

The average budgie owner may have his pet for its entire lifetime without its once needing any first aid treatment or minor surgery. Yet, judging from the number of these pets which we treated, accidents and ailments do occur which anyone with just a little love of nursing can easily treat with considerable assurance of success. Here are most of those which might call on your skill.

Nail and Beak Ailments. When the nails become too long and, by curling, interfere with the budgie's standing on a flat surface or properly grasping a round, cut them back to the proper length, which is about one-fourth of an inch. Use any strong scissors. If you have a dog or cat and own nail clippers for that pet, use those. Hold the bird with a strong light behind it and you can sometimes see the blood vessel and avoid cutting it.

If nails are broken and hanging, cut them off at the foot side of the break, as close to the break as possible, that is if it has not occured at the junction of the nail and toe, in which case simply cut off at the break. If you have cut too close and the nail bleeds, a touch with a styptic pencil will usually seal off the tiny blood vessel. If the toe is broken, it will often heal itself if you remove the nail entirely.

Beaks are frequently in need of shaping and shortening. One finds budgies with beaks which fail to function naturally as they should, which is with the lower mandible fitting just inside the upper. The mandibles, when in need of attention, may be in the reverse order—with the upper fitting inside the lower, or the upper may be so long the bird cannot lift it enough to make a mouth opening large enough to pick up its food. In rare instances the mandibles may not mesh at all, one growing sideways of the other.

Obviously, at the first sign of difficulty in eating, you should examine the beak and trim the proper mandible to conform to the natural state. Be sure to have a cuttlebone for your pet to keep its beak in condition. If it is twisted out of shape and you cannot repair the beak, take the bird to a specialist and let him attempt to fix it. But trimming is easy if you use strong scissors. Be careful, however, to avoid cutting into the live tissue. Remove the chalky excess growth, cutting back to the sound live horny tissue following the natural line of the bill.

Egg-bound. A female budgie with an egg stuck in the cloaca soon shows it by a loss of condition. The egg prevents the passage of feces with the urine and damming up of these products within the body results in toxemia, practically self-poisoning. The bird's feathers may appear ruffled and she does not sit in the nest as might be expected. She wears that "don't care" expression. Many budgie owners expect the egg-bound pet to appear to be straining to pass the egg, but the little hens do not strain to pass it; that process has been attempted in the nest box.

To determine if your bird is egg-bound, feel ever so gently on both sides of the cloaca and the egg will be identified. Having determined the obstruction, you may now try to ease it out as follows:

Draw some mineral oil into a smooth pointed medicine dropper and holding the bird upside down, gently push the dropper between the cloaca and the egg shell without breaking the shell. Encircle the egg, squeezing oil out as you do so.

If the hen cannot expel the egg now that the passage is no longer dry, she can only be saved by breaking the egg, letting the contents run out and squeezing the abdomen until the shell is crushed. This should only be used as a last resort, and should be attempted only by an experienced breeder or a veterinarian.

You may find another egg behind the first, in which case your efforts and the oil may enable the hen to pass it naturally. But if not, she will still need a veterinarian's attention.

She is not spoiled as a breeder by this experience. Many a hen has been egg-bound once and never again in her lifetime. Occasionally one finds a hen which repeatedly binds and such birds are not good stock for breeding.

Constipation. There is much difference between genuine constipation and the inability to defecate; yet ever so many bird owners do not realize

This opaline cin-
namon skyblue is a
very handsome blue
with good position.

This opaline cobalt
has excellent color,
markings, spots and
position, qualifying
him for exhibition.

A yellow face opaline mauve with beautiful coloring but a too deeply curved chest. Additionally, the bird's back is shaped too irregularly.

Skyblue is one of the colors most admired by bird lovers. The constant demand for size, large skull formation and giant spots has led to a type of showbird that sits, rather than stands, on the perch.

the fact. True constipation is an internal ailment and rare in budgies, in fact, on a wholesome diet almost never seen. Inability to defecate more often comes from a matting of feces on feathers which forms a constriction which prevents the passage of more feces. Sometimes egg-bound hens seem constipated.

The remedy for true constipation is as simple as giving a drop or two of mineral oil and thereafter feeding fruit and greens, also being sure the bird has a little gravel for its gizzard.

The remedy for formation of plugs or masses of feces on the feathers is simply pulling out or cutting off the feathers which are holding the mass in place. If the feces are stuck to the skin, apply warm water to soften the mass, or you may pull the bird's skin off with it. If an egg is plugging the cloaca, remove it (see egg-bound).

Diarrhea. This condition is usually associated with generalized sickness, but it can result from the feeding of laxative food. The feces appear watery, of various shades of color, unlike normal droppings. They may even be blood-tinged at times. The feathers around the rump are discolored, yellow or green, and in advanced cases, the feathers may be missing entirely.

Food diarrhea is cured by feeding properly, but other forms disappear when the disease is over. Two drops of milk of bismuth on the seed frequently has a miraculous effect. If the budgie is not eating, hold the bird and put the medicine into the sides of its mouth with a medicine dropper. This applies to all liquid medication. When abnormal bacteria in the intestines—those which may come with food—produce diarrhea, an antibiotic in the drinking water will eliminate them promptly.

Crop-bound. Budgies which eat coarse dry food or strings, paper, etc., may become crop-bound. The crop is a small storage reservoir holding food until the gizzard is empty. Naturally then, if the substance becomes matted into a more or less solid mass, it does not move on as it should. The material may become infected with bacteria which can live in such an environment and putrefy.

Mineral oil to soften the dried material and move it along should be the first treatment given. The crop lining is fairly tough so that gentle kneading is not harmful to the bird. Kneading mixes the oil with the food, which can then pass downward, a little at a time.

If this treatment fails, surgery by a veterinarian is called for.

Wound Treatment. Usually it is necessary only to clean the wound and clip the feathers around it. Pulling feathers from a wound already painful only adds to the bird's misery. If the wound is superficial, apply peroxide and keep it clean. If the wound is deep in the muscles, better give an antibiotic by mouth. Aureomycin in the drinking water will be excellent.

If the skin is torn deeply and appears to require sutures, apply an antiseptic and take the bird to a veterinarian.

Tumor Surgery. Budgies occasionally have lumps which develop rapidly. We have seen them on wings, in breast muscles, on a leg and in the neck. Surgery by a veterinarian is called for.

Setting Broken Bones. The trick of setting a broken bone is to be sure the ends are together. It requires two persons to set a leg bone in budgies but wing bones can be set by one person, although two do it more efficiently.

If the wing bone is broken, fold the wing in its natural position against the body with the bone ends touching and wind a one-inch gauze strip about the body, and under the other wing. Some strips of half-inch wide adhesive tape will hold the gauze bandage in place. This jacket must remain on the bird two and one half to three weeks, after which time the bone will be joined and lime deposited at the break to make it rigid. If you remove it too soon, the ends may be joined but not rigid and the wing will lie against the body abnormally, or actually become twisted.

Leg breaks can be set with tiny plaster casts. Your druggist will supply you with the plaster. We prefer Johnson's Duo Adhesive to set birds' legs. This comes in a tube. If you use it, apply a thick layer to the leg which your assistant is holding stretched enough so the bone ends are in place. As the adhesive is setting, press three half-length flat toothpicks into it and then apply a little more adhesive. Now wind a narrow strip of thin handkerchief linen around so that it sticks to the adhesive. You will have made a neat little cast.

Making one of plaster is only a matter of building up the wet plaster on the tiny leg. Winding thin linen around helps make it stronger and you must hold the bird until the plaster is completely set. Allow the cast to remain in place two and one half weeks at least.

Removing either variety of cast is tedious and requires great care not to cut or injure the leg. Vinegar helps soften plaster; vanishing cream softens the Duo Adhesive.

Shock. The condition known as shock is produced in a variety of ways in birds. Fright, injuries, chilling or exhaustion may be responsible. Your budgie will breathe rapidly and may lie on its side or cling to the cage bars. If it knows you, pick it up and try to get it to stand on your finger, that is unless it is exhausted or chilled. We have seen budgies go into shock when a stranger trimmed their beaks and have seen them

This budgie (coloration normal gray) with long feathers, nicknamed a "duster," is one of the latest mutations, although the first mutation was on display at the Essendon Society's Annual Show in Kensington City Hall in England in 1960.

This picture shows that the budgie starts brooding before the clutch is completed. This explains why the young birds are so different in size.

recover quickly when the owner reached into the cage and had the bird stand on the owner's finger for four or five minutes.

If the budgie is bruised, chilled or exhausted, keep it warm and talk to it. Holding it in your hands is often quite effective because you establish confidence and warm it at the same time.

Chilling—Overheating. In either of these conditions, do not carry your pet to the opposite extreme to save it. A chilled budgie needs warmth but not too much; an overheated budgie needs to be cooled but not too suddenly. Take it where it can breathe cooler air and its temperature will drop. There is no need to hold it under the cold water faucet as one owner we know did. There generally is value, however, in furnishing cool drinking water to help reduce the bird's temperature.

Feather Troubles. Because they are most obvious, feather abnormalities are noticed at once. Only a few feathers out of place produce a ragged appearance to the eye of a budgie connoisseur.

One of the most common feather troubles is a habit which some birds have of pulling out their own feathers. Some eat them but most budgies drop them on the floor of the cage. We are not always sure why they do it. Infestations with mites or other parasites is often the cause. Occasionally we find a budgie with everything right about it; no parasites, excellent conditions, plenty of protein foods, and still the bird pulls feathers.

One remedy consists of reducing the temperature of its living quarters. This nearly always stops it. Another remedy is furnishing more things for the bird to do. Another is to give more flying space. We have known a budgie to stop feather pulling when it was given a mate.

Broken feathers do not grow in until the shaft has been pulled out. Not until the molt can you expect new feathers. Suppose, therefore, you are buying a bird with clipped wings or your own budgie breaks off several of its wing or tail feathers. Pull the broken or cut shafts and new ones will shortly come in.

Coprophagy. Eating of droppings is usually indulged in by birds on inadequate diets. It becomes a habit, however, and a most annoying one. The cure seems to be to arrange a wire mesh floor in the cage, through which droppings will fall. This removes droppings from the reach of the bird. Besides the wire bottom, adequate, abundant diet may produce a permanent cure.

Poisoning. Budgies, like any other animal with curiosity, occasionally eat what they should not. Fresh paint is one of those things. "Mouse Knots" (small packages of poisoned grain) are another. Poison on lettuce leaves is yet another. Birds are especially susceptible to nicotine poisoning, so all fresh greens which might have been sprayed should be carefully washed.

Treatment consists in physicking your budgie as soon after it has eaten the offending or poisonous substance as possible. Because it is alkaline and a fair antidote for several poisons, milk of magnesia is a good physic in poison cases. Give the bird half a medicine dropperful.

Besides all these first aid treatments it is not at all uncommon to be called on to treat such occurrences as bruising when an escaped budgie flies into the wall and collapses in a pile of feathers on the floor. One budgie fell into a soup pot on the stove, was very quickly retrieved, rinsed under the water faucet and lived.

Many a pet has wound itself up in a long string and screamed for help or exhausted itself. Others have been kept in cages whose bars were too far apart, and have stuck their heads out between two bars but were unable to pull back. One of our clients ran for a neighbor to help her extract her bird and when the two returned the budgie was dead, whereas, had the woman not grown panicky, she could have pulled the thin bars apart and saved the valuable little fellow.

Most of the unforeseen accidents need only a little common sense to treat them successfully.